Cumberland Gold

JIMMY WHEELER

PAGE PUBLISHING, INC.
Conneaut Lake, PA

First originally published by Page Publishing 2021

This book is a work of fiction. Names, characters, places, and incidents are the product of the author's imagination or are used fictitiously. Locales and public names are sometimes used for atmospheric purposes. Any resemblance to actual people, living or dead, or to businesses, companies, events, institutions, or locales is completely coincidental.

Credits:
Typing-Jacob Williamson
Photography-Benjamin Galland

ISBN 978-1-6624-2001-6 (pbk)
ISBN 978-1-6624-2002-3 (digital)

Printed in the United States of America

CHAPTER 1

The History of Cumberland Island (According to Bo Sam)

"A treasure on Cumberland Island? Heck yeah, and I know three places where it could be!" Wilder and Mark knew why everyone who met Captain Bo Sam called him BS for short because every story he told was worth a little embellishing. He had shared some of his collection of artifacts, which he had found on the island, including old military buttons, a musket, other brass buttons, and his most valuable item—a sword. He had found these using his state of the art Garmin metal detector he had paid $1,500 for on eBay. The boys told him they had developed their own theory where to find gold coins and had been given a primitive map that would lead them to the treasure. BS told them they had been watching too much of the *Curse of Oak Island*, which was a popular series on the History channel. His suggestion to them was to call the brothers who had spent millions of dollars and invite them to help them since the Oak Island treasure located in the "money pit" had not been located in two hundred years.

He told them they should write a book and call it, *Curse of Cumberland Island* because almost everything built there had either burned like the Dungeness mansion or disappeared like the forts built on the north and south ends of the island. If these two lads could blend in with the other thirty-five residents of the island, they knew they had a better chance. They were eager to begin—more about that later.

"Wanna go to Cumberland Island and catch some trout, reds, and flounder?" Captain Richard asked his two friends, who were recent UGA grads—all they had to do is bring a cooler full of Bud Light and some extra crispy fried chicken.

Mark and Wilder both had this trip on their "bucket list" and agreed to meet at Jointer Creek Marina the next morning at 5:30 a.m. Captain Bo Sam (who was called Cap BS by his fisherman friends) was hooking up the new, sleek twenty-four-foot Sea Pro with a four-stroke 300 hp Yamaha to the boat hoist while singing one of his hero's favorite tunes, "Margaritaville" by Jimmy Buffett. The boat was lowered until it was in the water, and the crew took their coolers, rods and reels, ice, and three quarts of lively Georgia white shrimp for the baitwell. As his customary standard operating procedure, he asked the crew about their destination and ETA back at the marina. Everyone knew BS had made numerous trips to rescue fishermen who experienced problems such as running out of gas, dead batteries, or getting lost, especially in the fog. He monitored channel 16 at his home base VHF, and everyone had his cell number. After Captain Richard had completed his boaters checklist, he told BS it was hammer downtime for a

Christmas Creek fishing trip. BS was telling the crew about how the sandbars had recently shifted, and it was a real challenge to get into the creek, especially at low tide.

Captain Richard had a few rules for those lucky enough to fish on his new twenty-four-foot Sea Pro—absolutely no junk scattered anywhere. He furnished tackle for everyone, which consisted of Penn Battle reels and rods which were spooled with 20-pound braided line and there were cork rigs, bottom rigs, or rigs to use with artificial bait. They cruised at a comfortable 42 mph and only slowed, as they were passing an anchored boat or a stationary dock. Once they passed Jekyll Island on the riverside, they reached St. Andrews Sound. The captain pulled back on the throttle and explained they would be going to the ocean side of the island to see if they could spot some tripletail and maybe catch one. He explained that these fish are seen floating on their side and look like a trash can lid floating on the top of the water. When Captain Richard thought he saw one, he turned off the main engine and deployed his GPS trolling motor to be in stealth mode. Two minutes later, he cast a small cork rig baited with a live shrimp 3 feet in front of the floating fish, and *bam*, big fish on!

Braided line peeled from the Battle 3000 reel, and he shouted for Mark to follow the fish with the trolling motor, which became a disaster since he had no idea what to do with the remote. Wilder, who had used one once, turned the motor to follow the fish, which was now 60 feet from the boat. The fight lasted for ten minutes, and then the 12-pound tripletail came to the surface and was netted. Captain Richard explained that these three tailed fish were delicious, especially on the grill and were often the featured "catch of the day" fish on the menu of some of his favorite restaurants like Georgia Sea Grille and Halyards Restaurant, both located on St. Simons Island. They grilled or blackened a nice thick fillet, and then their presentation was superb—a nice white sauce often topped with cherry tomatoes, asparagus, small red potatoes, or many other items in their recipe guide.

The captain told his two mates that he often practiced "catch and release," but today they were fishing to have a cookout, and the featured dish would be tripletail on the grill. So today would be "find and fillet!" He added that these fish show up in only two places on the eastern seaboard, floating on their side beginning in April through the summer months on the beach in front of Cape Canaveral, Florida, and right here in front of Jekyll Island, Georgia. He also mentioned an ole captain friend of his, Captain Jim, had told him the secret he had learned many years ago about how to catch the really giant ones 30-plus pounds after beach fishing is over. They both wanted to know, but when the amount of money it would take for him to tell them was revealed, they quit asking.

Captain Richard explained to the boys that there were two major obstacles to conquer because of the narrow channel created by an ever-changing sandbar. Since this was his first trip to this area this year, he did not have the new route in his GPS, and he would have to make a decision by examining the ripples in the water. He said, "Hold on, boys," and pushed down the throttle and trimmed up the motor and zoomed past some poor soul who had missed the channel by 10 feet and was "high and dry." They bumped the bottom once, but the experienced captain trimmed up the motor another few inches before clearing hurdle #1. Next would be to decide where to choose to run into the creek because of the many sandbars in front and the very skinny water conditions. He gave the same orders and did the same thing as before, bumping twice at the speed of 55 mph. Once inside, the boys were wide-eyed and asked the captain how he was able to make those two perilous runs and not hit a sandbar, and Captain Richard smiled and replied, "I have no idea. My eyes were closed both times because I was praying!"

No other boats were in the creek probably because of the low water conditions, which was ideal since they could work the mouth of the creek with the trolling motor on low speed, or when the anchor button was pressed on the remote, the boat would remain in one spot, compensating for the wind and current. Captain Richard said they would be trying to catch trout, reds, flounder, and whiting. They had three baits: live shrimp, mud minnows, and plastic. He said that fishing with a minnow on the bottom was deadly for flounder, and that technique was the reason he had earned the shirt he was wearing, which read, "Flounder Pounder." He then hooked a fat minnow through both lips and cast it toward the bank while helping the boys with their cork rigs baited with live shrimp.

Captain Richard saw his rod tip twitch, and he knew a flounder was having a nice meal on the bottom of the creek, so he counted to fifteen and tightened the line, felt a heavy weight, and then set the hook. The two-toned flatfish made the drag scream as it tried to pull the hook. Meanwhile, the boys each had a "go down" on their cork rigs and were each reeling in a pair of nice speckled trout to the boat. Captain Richard managed to net both trout and then his flounder of about 3 pounds. They all had a good laugh at this "Chinese fire drill" and knew this was the start of a day to remember. Everyone caught their limit of trout, and they had two flounder, each with one being a 5-pound "doormat." The tide started running too swift where they were fishing and Captain Richard decided to have some fun with "catch and release" at his favorite secret redfish drop. They used a variety of grub/jig combinations to catch over thirty nice 3- to 5-pound reds, and Mark told his buddies his arm was tired, and he declared the time to be "beer thirty!" Everyone agreed and enjoyed an ice-cold Bud Light and some dead chicken from KFC.

Wilder asked the captain if they could exit the creek and ride down the beach south toward Lake Whitney and catch some whiting since he had told his neighbor, Cotton Lee, that he would bring him some fresh "whitin" as he called them. He said he would have a fish fry for them and invite Captain Bo Sam to provide entertainment for everyone. As they rode slowly down the beach, they spotted a lady on a four-wheeler, examining a dead turtle that had washed up on the beach. They decided to fish in front of a Lake Whitney "run out," which was usually a productive whiting drop. The lady was only a few yards away, so Captain Richard began chatting with her and soon realized she was the legendary "Wild Woman of Cumberland Island," who was said to live on the island in a cabin she built by hand close to the African Baptist Church where the Kennedy wedding took place. It was rumored that she ate roadkill, wrestled alligators, rode wild horses bareback, and had shot and killed her husband, who she told the Camden

County sheriff, Mark Proctor, had attacked her, and it was done in self-defense. Captain Richard told his crew to start fishing for whiting by throwing toward the ocean instead of the beach because the whiting were in deeper water, and trout were near the beach. They had already reached their limit for trout and now could catch all the great tasting little kingfish they wanted.

The captain watched the lady named Maggie use her buck knife to dissect the dead turtle and put the remains in a ziplock bag. She said the death was probably caused by it drowning in a shrimp net being pulled along the beach by one of the many shrimp trawlers. She said she never understood why the DNR allowed them to shrimp so close to the beach, but it was pure and simple politics. The boys had managed to catch fifty or sixty whiting, and before leaving, he asked Maggie if she wanted a mess of fish to cook, and she laughed and said four or five would be fine for her. He gave her two flounder and three trout. She said she was going to eat mighty fine tonight! She left on her four-wheeler, and Wilder and Mark began formulating their next adventure to the island, and little did they know it would be the start of a wild ride for them. This trip would change their lives forever. Now hold on to your hats. The ride is just beginning!

"We got this," Wilder told Mark as the two made their way without Captain Richard. Their plan was to take their camping gear in their jon boat and explore the island concentrating on the north end—Little Cumberland Island. They were greeted at the marina by BS, and he laughed when he saw how their boat was loaded and asked them where they would sit because it was packed full. They had a tent, flashlights, lanterns, a large tackle box, food, water, and, of course, a case of Bud Light. Six rod and reels were balanced on their canvas bags, which contained their clothing.

When they asked BS how long it would take them to get to Christmas Creek, he grinned and told them it depended on how fast they ran in choppy water and how many sandbars they got stuck on. Their ETA was about 7:00 a.m., and they felt confident because they had borrowed a handheld GPS that neither was sure how to use. BS asked the boys what their plan was if it was too rough in Saint Andrews Sound for their sixteen-foot boat, and both replied, "We will turn around and come back here and drink beer with you! Same as coming out in three days—may have to wait it out."

The boat was launched, the motor cranked, and the adventure had begun! BS told them as they were leaving that he was going down to an insurance agency and take out a million-dollar policy on them. They saw no humor in that smart remark.

Their plan was to reach the mouth of the creek on the first of incoming tide for two reasons. First, they would not have to wait a long time if they got stuck on a sandbar, and second was they wanted to see the creek when the tide was low to get a visual of where the sandbars were located. The weather was perfect, seas were calm, and they made it past the lighthouse with no problem. At the mouth of the creek, they slowed down to a stop to inspect the route, and Wilder remembered what his buddy, Captain Jim, had once told him, "Always remember, time and tide wait for no man!"

A decision was made to get up on a plane and give it all she had like Captain Richard had done, and because of a slight miscalculation, they hit a sandbar, and the motor flew up in the air and gave them a nice shower of salt water and sand. They determined that their GPS was no good to them because it had not been programmed for the route into the creek, and both wished their motor had been equipped with a trim and tilt to allow them to raise and lower it like Captain Richard had done. The good news was the tide was coming in fast, and they only had to wait twenty minutes to pull the small boat off and try again but still not enough water with the motor down, so they pushed and pulled until they found the channel and decided to go slow this time for safety's sake. Mark asked Wilder as they put it along if he felt something touch him while they were in the water, and he said, "Yes, probably just a shark. These are the most shark-infested waters south of Chesapeake Bay." Mark wasn't sure if he was kidding or not, but he did file this bit of information in his almost full memory bank.

"Hooray! We made it in the creek!" Mark shouted as they saw the spot they had fished with Captain Richard. They had bought some live shrimp at the marina but decided to throw their cast net and try to catch some mullet and minnows to use for flounder. On the last trip, they had seen a small saltwater pond on the right just inside the creek, so they beached their boat and headed toward it. All they needed was a 5-gallon bucket and their net to get the bait. The first cast made hundreds of mullet jump into the air, and a few were still under the net when Mark shook it into the bucket. Wilder noticed a big log moving in their direction, but it had eyes and a tail. He told his buddy that this pond belonged to that ten-foot critter swimming toward them, and they should start heading for the boat because it may want some free mullet they just caught. The gator got closer, and Wilder remembered what he had learned from Captain Jim, "Them creatures can outrun a human." They did not walk back to the boat. They ran and never looked back to see if the log was following them. They jumped in the boat they had nicknamed "Mad Minnow" and went to their fishing drop.

"Been here fifteen minutes and almost got eaten by a shark and a gator. What could happen next to top that?" Mark said. (Just wait, rookies!)

The boys planned to catch enough fish to cook on their two-burner Coleman grill they had brought, but this day was totally different. The water was not clear, and the fish had lockjaw! They voted to go to plan B, which was to catch a mess of those good-eating whiting at a drop in the back of the creek, where Captain Richard said catching them was so easy a blind monkey could do it. Sure enough, the bull whiting big enough to fillet were there, and fishing with a tiny piece of dead shrimp on the bottom produced ten of them. They left and headed back to a creek they had decided to explore and possibly camp in on the bank if no one saw them. They knew about park rangers enforcing the law, but they were not sure what the rules were, so they decided "better to ask forgiveness than beg permission." The salt water had been coming in for a while, and they entered the tiny creek, and after three curves, there it was— the perfect campsite covered with giant live oak trees and tall palm trees. They had made one huge mistake picking that creek but more about that later.

They pulled their small boat up on the bank and began to unload their tent and all the other gear. Since Cumberland Island is a national seashore, it was their plan to camp in a secluded spot since they had not asked anyone about the rules of camping there. They decided not to make a campfire because it might alert the park rangers to their location. Instead, they would use their two-burner Coleman portable grill to fry their fish and steam oysters and clams yet to be harvested.

Several lessons were learned that trip. They had chosen to camp in a zoo full of horses, deer, hogs, snakes, raccoons, possums, and many other critters! Some visited their campsite and tried to eat the groceries they brought. The boys decided to put the groceries in a large canvas bag and use a rope to hoist it up a tree to get it off the ground, where the critters roamed. Some of these varmints would even climb up the tree for a fresh Georgia tomato, and their solution was to tie a knot at the top that even Harry Houdini could not untie. They never knew a raccoon could open up a jar of mayonnaise with their tiny, nimble fingers, and wild hogs would not obey your command of "Get outta here!" no matter how hard you hollered! The first night, the hogs grunted, growled, and squealed. Later, they learned the grunt was made while foraging for food, the squeal denoted excitement or attempting to communicate being approached, and the growl meant aggression. The hogs must have been having a "welcome to the island" reception because all three sounds were heard during their camping trip. A sidenote—even a large monkey was said to be spotted by Wilder one night, but its presence still remains a mystery today.

Another lesson was to pick out a creek on low tide instead of a higher tide to ensure there was enough water to navigate in and out on the low tide. This was useful to prevent you from having to drag your boat in skinny water to reach the main channel—lesson learned quickly!

Lesson three is that the large red dot moving parallel to you while you are walking in the water gigging flounder is not a red Coke can when you shine your high-beam flashlight on it—no, that would be an alligator! This may contribute to making the UGA boys have so much disdain for their neighbors in Florida, who are gator fans, often performing the chomp-chomp with their arms at football games.

Several other lessons included having Band-Aids and Neosporin with you on your trip would be appreciated if you ever got a painful cut while picking wild oysters—a guarantee to happen! Also, always wear shoes while walking in the saltwater creeks. A sting from even a small stingray could send you to the emergency room. Another lesson would be unless you enjoy getting hit in the head by a flying mullet, don't shine your high-beam in open salt water at night. Put a sheet over your head and let them fall in the boat for you to eat later.

After three days of enjoying the island and learning some valuable lessons, they cleaned up their campsite and made it out to the main creek. The sun was just beginning to rise, and boats could be heard racing by the creek to be the first one to claim a prized fishing drop on the beach. Since they still had live bait and ample fuel, they employed their "monkey see, monkey do" philosophy and chose a spot on the beach that had a deep run out, which usually produced lots of action. By 9:30 a.m., they had filled up their cooler with nice 2-pound trout, but they were running low on ice. Another valuable fishing lesson learned—the earlier, the better when beach fishing. Usually, you will have your limit in a couple of hours. As they left the beach of Cumberland with its white powder sand glistening, Wilder and Mark did a high five and made a pact that they would return soon to their newly found island paradise.

Captain BS was at his marina, wearing one of his favorite T-shirts, which read, "I used to think drinking was bad for me, so I gave up thinking!" He offered the boys an ice-cold Bud Light, and they sat down, and when the story started, you could hear laughter across the marsh for miles. Wilder asked BS about the lady who rode the four-wheeler and examined dead animals she encountered on the beach. BS beamed as he exclaimed that he had met one of the strongest and most controversial ladies who had ever lived on the island. He called her Maggie because most of all the dead animals she found were full of maggots. She was the expert and most knowledgeable person on earth when it came to loggerhead turtles. He said he had formulated a module for a college class based on a lot of her research. He taught off campus for UGA. He volunteered to give them a quick lesson for free, and both agreed. He pulled out his flip board from the marina office, and four pages of turtle facts emerged.

Turtles are one of the oldest animal species on earth dating back over 230 million years. They have spread across every continent except Antarctica and have populated remote areas from mountaintops to ocean floors. Their blood acts like antifreeze, allowing them to tolerate extremely cold temperatures, and they can collapse their lungs and hold their breath for nine minutes, allowing them to dive a half-mile deep into the ocean. Their shell is their built-in condo, and this bony box formed over millions of years as their ribs widened and fused together. Their shells have nerves, and if injured, the turtles bleed, and it is believed they feel pain.

All turtles, tortoises, and terrapins have shells. Tortoises live on dry land, turtles live mostly in water, and terrapins live in brackish marshes like the one surrounding the Golden Isles of Georgia. He added that several of the beautiful terrapins march out of the marsh the same time each year, lay their eggs, and return to the marsh. BS noted that one had dug her nest under the marina at the same spot for the past six years. It is rumored that some local idiots kill these beautiful creatures for their diamond back shell.

There are seven species of sea turtles and five nest on Cumberland Island. The leatherbacks are the largest and have a unique "third eye"—a signal receiving splotch on their forehead, which acts as a compass in navigation. They make the longest migration across the Atlantic and return to nest on the same beaches where they were born. Some tagged ones, who hatched on the island, traveled across the Atlantic and returned thirty years later to their birthplace to lay their eggs. The sea turtles don't travel in groups. Instead, they travel solo. They travel one mile per hour, swimming through kelp forests and amazing coral reefs. They are fortunate to escape all the toothed fish that lurk in these waters, including sharks, giant tuna, and marlin. When they reach the Gulf Stream, a giant river that circulates clockwise from the Caribbean to Europe, they ride the five-mile-per-hour current eastward across the Atlantic Ocean. The turtles have to surface every five minutes to take a quick breath because they are the most ancient marine creatures that have to breathe air. When they reach the Sargasso Sea, which is in the Bermuda Triangle, they gorge on small shrimp and plankton and sleep in the grass beds. The water is clear and blue, and the winds are generally calm.

The brown seaweed, sargassum, can live for hundreds of years and provides shelter for turtles until their shells become hard, and they leave in search of their favorite food, jellyfish. About ten years old and about the size of a dinner plate, the turtles begin the four-thousand-mile journey to the warm waters of the coast of Africa. Some of these turtles will return to Cumberland and lay their eggs in the dunes on the beach—a truly extraordinary species that makes one of the world's extraordinary adventures.

Captain BS told his captive audience that they needed to know about the history of the island if they planned to locate any treasure left there by the early settlers. His chart revealed that Cumberland Island is the largest of Georgia's barrier islands that protect the mainland from storms and hurricanes. It is eighteen miles long and ranges from three to three and one-half miles in width. Its 36,000 acres makes it a third larger than Manhattan. History records reveal Spanish missions there in the sixteenth century, and that two-forts were laid out by General James Oglethorpe in the 1730s, one on the south end and one on the north. Planters brought slaves to the island, and prestigious families such as Nathaniel Greene became interested in the island's natural resources, and the first mansion was built on the island and called Dungeness. Long before the slave owners, the first Europeans were French Calvinists who arrived on Cumberland Island in 1562. They were French-speaking Protestants who discovered the peaceful and quite handsome Timucuan Indians. These Indians knew the island as Tacatacuru, meaning "beautiful island." The tribe was much larger than the French, with some of the men over seven feet tall and some women over six feet. They worshipped the sun and the moon and sometimes only wore Spanish moss for clothing. Many of the men and some of the women covered most of their bodies with elaborate mazelike tattoos made by slicing their dark skin and rubbing soot in the bleeding wounds. They ate mostly oysters, fish, acorns, roots, and deer meat.

In 1733, Colonel James Oglethorpe from Savannah founded Darien, Georgia, to use as a buffer between the Spanish and the people of Savannah. In 1736, he established Fort Frederica on St. Simons Island. In the same year, he went on an expedition to Cumberland Island with the proud Indian chief Tomochichi and his young nephew Toonahowi, who suggested that the island be called Cumberland.

In 1748, the island became a neutral territory between Spain and England and a refuge for criminals, debtors, and deserters from both sides. Captain Bo Sam had all these facts and dates written on his flip chart, which he put on an easel. He bragged that he made his "beer money" from lectures he gave various groups and college classes because he was known throughout the South as the "Cumberland Island master historian."

He pointed out that a group known as "Grey's Gang," led by Quaker Edmund Grey in 1757, guided this group of three hundred to the island and engaged in small trade with Spain and India for eight to ten years. This was the first semipermanent settlement on the island. The captain then pointed out the date of 1776, and he asked them what significant war happened then, and their answer was the Revolutionary War. He added that the island was mostly abandoned, but the British occupied it for a staging area before the attack on Savannah in 1778.

The year 1783 showed General Nathaniel Greene purchasing land on Cumberland Island for timber harvesting, hoping that money made from the timber would pay off his immense debt. He died of sunstroke in 1786 and left all his property to his wife Catherine Greene and their children. BS paused and said, "Too much sun will take away your fun!"

Caty, as her friends called her, was rumored to flirt with some very important gentlemen, including George Washington, commander in chief, and her husband's very unpredictable fellow officer General Anthony Wayne, who was called "Mad Anthony." She also had the attention of Eli Whitney, who she inspired to invent the machine to separate cotton seeds from lint, which we know as the cotton gin. Since cotton was so labor-intensive, this invention made Coastal Georgia the "cotton capital."

BS asked the boys if they wanted to learn more about Cumberland Island, and both were eager to learn more. The plan was to return in two days and help with the repair of the live bait tank and soak up some more island knowledge. Mark had other obligations, but Wilder jumped at the opportunity and agreed to meet at the marina in two days at 7:00 a.m.

When Wilder returned, he saw the words "Yazoo Affair" written on the chart, and BS began telling him the story of a colossal land scheme that happened in 1795. It involved Caty and her second husband Phineas Miller. Miller was the man she chose over other suitors, including George Washington and Eli Whitney. He had been a tutor for her five children—George, Martha, Cornelia, Nat, and Louisa. Strong and reserved, he was Yale-educated and was a man of culture and manners. He was ten years younger than Caty, and he instantly fell in love with her, but initially, she just liked his companionship. The plan was to buy 35 million acres of undeveloped land from the Georgia legislature and sell it to cotton planters who were coming to the state at a great profit. The land comprised most of present-day Alabama and Mississippi. They were to pay $490,000 for the land, but the word got out, and the citizens of Georgia convinced the newly elected legislature to rescind the corrupt deal the next year. Facing bankruptcy, Caty devised a plan to grow cotton on the island, which had rich soil conducive to growing cotton. Her husband was also cutting live oaks growing on Cumberland Island to sell to New England shipyards. Some of this oak was used to build the hull of the ship USS *Constitution*, helping it win the nickname "Old Ironsides" because the oak wood was almost as strong as iron.

Because of the success of the cotton business, Caty began to design her dream home located on the south end of the island, which would be called Dungeness. It had a tabby exterior covered with oyster shells. These shells were left by the Timucuan Indians, who ate oysters as part of their diet and built mounds with the shells. The thirty-room house was ninety feet tall with sixteen fireplaces. It was surrounded by a twelve-acre garden containing thousands of flowers, trees, and shrubs. The garden had eight hundred olive trees as well as sago palms, coffee plants, orange trees, lime trees, fig trees, pomegranate, and guava trees. The couple moved into what was then called the most elegant home on the Georgia coast in 1803. Caty's second husband had the misfortune of puncturing his finger on a trip to Florida to buy tropical plants and died of lockjaw at the age of thirty-nine.

Caty continued to oversee Dungeness, and lavish parties were attended by such notables as Eli Whitney, who with other guests, feasted on fresh fish, crabs, oysters, duck, geese, and venison. Also, Caty's specialty of brandy-soaked peaches and watermelon rind pickles were enjoyed by all. For restful nights, a keg of rum was kept for hot toddies at bedtime. Guests fished, hunted, had picnics, rode horses on the beach, and enjoyed cards, dancing, and musical performances in the evenings. Caty lived to be only sixty years old. In August 1814, she caught malaria and died in her sleep.

BS who was proud to call himself a Raconteur, teller of funny and interesting stories, told Wilder it was time for recess, so they decided to take a break, grab a few cold beers, and boat out to Jointer Creek to catch some bait shrimp, which were now fetching $15 a quart which yielded a nice profit. BS chuckled and said that those big ole "chicken leg" shrimp were too big to fish with but would be great grilled or cooked in a low country boil he planned to create when they got back to the marina. BS showed Wilder how to deploy the shrimp nets from the nineteen-foot Carolina skiff, which had been converted to his bait boat. He explained the purpose of the "tickler chain" on the bottom of the wooden doors—they "tickled" the shrimp, which were on the mud creek bottom to come up from the mud and get caught in the net. He told Wilder one could hear a tiny laugh made by these "tickled" shrimp when dumped out of the net. After only twenty minutes of pulling the net, the small Briggs and Stratton motor was cranked and pulled the net up to the boat and was constantly shook by BS to get all the shrimp to the bottom of the net. Hundreds of shrimp and other creatures were in the net, ready to be separated into the good, the bad, and the ugly. Edible fish were kept such as trout and whiting, but most of the bycatch were thrown back into the creek to survive if not eaten by the flock of pelicans hovering over the boat.

A long open-ended tray had been fiberglassed in the boat, and the net was emptied on it, and BS's hands moved like magic, picking the shrimp out and throwing them in the baitwell. He said to always watch for the stingrays because they could inflict a nasty wound if they hit you with their tail and could possibly send you to the emergency room. He said even Steve Irvin, known as the "Crocodile Hunter," died while swimming with rays. BS put the "chicken legs" size shrimp on ice since they had so graciously volunteered to jump in the net—next jump would be in the low country boil.

Wilder decided shrimping was a lot like fishing. Knowing where to go, when to go, and having the right equipment separate the successful captains from the others. Two more drags produced all the shrimp they could legally keep, and they returned to the marina two hours later. The live shrimp were put in the live bait well at the marina, and BS shouted for Wilder to start getting the low country boil underway by cutting up some corn, potatoes, sausage, and rutabagas. Everything would be put into one large pot full of water (and two Bud Lights) with salt, pepper, Old Bay seasoning, garlic powder, and a generous dose of Louisiana hot sauce. For appetizers, BS threw in a few freshly caught blue crabs and a dozen eggs. Last to take the plunge in the hot water would be the shrimp, which would have only a five-minute bath. Wilder remarked that there was enough food to feed twenty-five people, and BS replied the "bluff boys" would be there like they were almost every day at 5:00 p.m. If some arrived early, they would point to a sign tacked on the wall that read, "It's five somewhere!"

They began to arrive in trucks, golf carts, and a few made in America Harley-Davidsons, better known as "hogs." They all said they would rather walk than ride one of "them foreign bikes!" Catfish was first to arrive, wearing his favorite Evil Knievel T-shirt, showing him jumping a line of cars on his bike. Slim arrived next, wearing a T-shirt that read, "I love my pork pulled and my butt rubbed!" John Earl was next, wearing his favorite "I pee in pools!" Billy Ray had one that read, "When I said, 'How stupid can you be?' it wasn't a challenge!"

Twenty more arrived, and they each had at least a twelve pack of cold beer, and John Earl was booed when he emptied his Hamm's beer in the big cooler. BS said he would not feed that horse piss to a dog dying of thirst! The boys ate like they hadn't eaten in a week, and the sausage and rutabagas were the first to be gone. BS had a few zip-lock bags for a "to-go" treat, except for John Earl. BS told his guests that since he and Wilder had cooked, they had to clean, but the job was easy with one pot to clean, and the newspaper the boil was poured on thrown away. BS told Wilder that CI 101 would resume the next morning at 7:00 a.m. sharp.

The captain had written 1818 on the chart and asked Wilder if they had ever heard of General "Light Horse" Harry Lee (father of General Robert E. Lee and subordinate to General Nathaniel Greene). Wilder, who had attended the University of Georgia and joined Kappa Alpha Order, was proud to say yes and was a dedicated student of the Civil War, especially Robert E. Lee. Harry had arrived at the island ill with cancer and was placed under the care of Caty's daughter Louisa Shaw. He died two months later and was buried at the little family cemetery at Dungeness. In 1832, his eldest son, Major Robert E. Lee, sent a head-stone to mark the grave.

Louisa Shaw also died at Dungeness and willed her estate to her nephew Phineas Miller Nightingale, who sold most of his holdings to Robert Stafford Jr. Stafford now became the largest plantation owner on the island, which has now become mostly developed plantations with numerous slaves.

The Dungeness mansion burned right after the Civil War when Union troops occupied the island. They were drinking rum and partying with the freed slaves the night that it caught fire and burned. A second mansion was built by Lucy Coleman Carnegie on the same spot as the original mansion. Before the second mansion was built, a beautiful mulatto slave named Zabette had four beautiful daughters fathered by none other than Robert Stafford, who was the biggest land and slave owner on the island. All the daughters eventually married royalty, including admirals and artists.

Robert Stafford, his sisters, and mother made their first large land buy on the island in 1813 when they bought nearly 600 acres for $3,000. This was the nucleus of what is still known today as Stafford Island. Stafford, who called himself a private banker, obtained another 4,200 acres at a sheriff's sale in St. Mary's, Georgia—for debt nonpayment from none other than Phineas Nightingale, who stilled lived at Dungeness. Stafford had acquired 8,000 acres on the island, and as the consummate entrepreneur, he sold the island's wild ponies for five dollars each to anyone brave enough to try to break them. The ponies had to swim from the island to the mainland, and they were driven by "horse dogs" that would bite any animal that tried to reverse course and swim back to the island. He used his strongest slaves to compete in rowing contests at St. Mary's, and his team usually won, making him lots of money.

Captain BS announced his throat hurt from all the talking he was doing and was in serious need of an ice-cold Bud Light. He told the boys he was going on a much-needed fishing trip with his new honey he fondly called sugar baby but whose real name was Catherine. She had never been to Louisiana, and since she loved fishing, she was in for the trip of a lifetime. They would leave at five the next morning for the ten-hour trip to Delacroix, Louisiana, where they would meet up with Captain Wendell and fish for three days. He explained that the fishing there was some of the best in the world, and the limits for trout and reds were very kind to all anglers with each keeping twenty-five trout and ten reds each. His previous eight trips there had been so productive that limits were usually caught by ten each morning, and then it was "catch and release," using artificial baits usually in the LSU purple and gold. He laughed when he explained how he and Cat would be forced to stop on the way back to do a little gambling at his favorite spot on the coast called the Beau Rivage Hotel in Biloxi, Mississippi. He would be playing with "free money" since it would be his winnings for catching a limit of trout first each day and the largest red. He said no one should ever bet against him in a fishing contest because he never lost! He bragged he was also known as a winning poker player, and the dealer at the Texas Holdem table dreaded to see him sit at their table.

BS was back at the marina the next Friday and had a big smile on his face when he greeted Wilder. Wilder asked him if he had fallen in love on his fishing trip with Cat, and he smiled and replied he had fallen in "heat," not love. He proceeded to light up a small Black and Mild cigar, which he claimed was one of the best methods to keep the sand gnats away, and said he loved to watch them Yankees fight "no-see-ums" when they came to the coast. Wilder asked him if today would be the day he learned more about the gold treasure, and BS told him he would get that information when the time was right and after he had learned more about the island and its history. He had written "The Civil War" on the chart and began his lecture while puffing on his little cigar.

He began by stating the Civil War began in 1861 and was responsible for laying waste to Cumberland Island's plantations. The planters returned to their former homes and found little of the order and peace they had known before the war. Fields were full of weeds, and houses, as well as farm buildings, were rotted and often falling down. The North emerged as a region of industrialization that was perfect for fortunes to be made. In 1886, a group of a hundred industrialists and financiers such as William Rockefeller, Frank Goodyear, Richard Crane, JP Morgan, William Vanderbilt, Joseph Pulitzer, and others bought Jekyll Island, Georgia, for $125,000. They formed the Jekyll Island Club, and its members represented one-sixth of the world's wealth. They built cottages of fifteen to twenty-five rooms, tennis courts, a swimming pool, a clubhouse, and a chapel that looked like it was copied from Notre Dame. They vacationed and partied there for fifty-six years until World War II began, and they decided to sell Jekyll to the State of Georgia in 1947. Several millionaires bought real estate on the barrier islands of Georgia, including Howard Coffin, founder of Detroit's Hudson Motor Company. He later developed Retreat Plantation on St. Simons Island with a championship golf course. On the now exclusive Sea Island, he and his cousin Albert W. Jones built the exclusive Cloister Hotel as a winter resort for the rich and famous. Pittsburg's steel magnate, Thomas Morrison Carnegie, and his wife Lucy Coleman Carnegie wanted their own island, and they chose Cumberland.

BS announced it was break time, and now would be a good time to get in the boat and go up the creek since it was the favorable low tide. He asked Wilder if he had ever harvested oysters from the wild, and he said no, but he had bought a ton over the years from City Market in Brunswick, Georgia. BS said the oysters they were going to pick had once been part of an oyster farming experiment, and in the twentieth century, Georgia had produced over 8,000,000 pounds every year to sustain its thriving oyster canning industry. It was reported by the National Oceanic and Atmospheric Administration that in the 1940s, the overharvesting and declining appetite for canned oysters led to the industry's demise. Recently, to revive the local oyster industry, lawmakers in Georgia passed a piece of legislation that would establish a framework for harvesters to start and operate oyster farms. Every coastal state has a money-making oyster business except for Georgia, which is dumb lamented BS.

He said that currently, only wild oyster harvesting was legal in Georgia, but unlike farmed oysters, wild oysters posed unique challenges for the consumers and restaurants. For one, wild ones grew in unruly clumps, which were often hard to separate, split, and serve. Also, their shape was inconsistent, and restaurants demanded single large oval-shaped oysters. They could then easily charge $15 per dozen for raw or steamed, which translated to a nice profit for them. Farming allowed harvesters to raise oysters in the same coastal waters that wild ones grow in while maintaining control over their shape. The baby oysters were regularly tumbled like bingo balls in a metal cage to keep them round and cupped. BS stated he supported government backing of oyster farming since the government provides farming on land with incentives that have been very beneficial for farmers. Why not have Georgia doing what little

South Carolina was doing by bringing in 2.29 million in revenue in 2015? In Florida, where the Apalachicola reigns supreme, revenue was 4.43 million in 2015!

He added that there was now a considerable debate in Georgia regarding the months a farmer could harvest his oysters—the push was to limit the number of months and exclude the summer months because of health concerns. Raw oyster consumption had been linked to a disease called vibriosis, which causes stomach problems and can be fatal for the elderly and young children. The risk was believed to be greater in the hot summer months.

Remember the saying "Eat oysters only in the months with an 'R' in them," which excluded May, June, July, and August. Actually, with the improvements in the oyster aquaculture and the availability of ice to keep them cold, this was no longer a valid reason. Oyster farmers in Florida and South Carolina were permitted to harvest all year long with no health issues. Georgia's oyster farmers would automatically face an economic and operational disadvantage. Another hurdle to overcome is how leases would be distributed—by lottery or open to not only Georgia but also states like Florida and South Carolina. Common sense said drop the debate and get on with an industry that will produce millions in revenue for Georgia and would create jobs for those who are tough enough to do this backbreaking work.

"Enough talking. Let's go gitter done!" hollered BS, who sounded like the current LSU football coach with that famous hoarse voice… Ed O?

BS showed his student what was necessary to get a bushel of those pearls of the sea-gloves, a claw hammer, and a croker sack. You also had to have some white rubber crabber boots to protect your feet. BS chuckled when he pointed out that it was a law in Coastal Georgia for the boots to be any color except white—the only exception was when a fellow crabber died, then you could wear black crabbing boots to his funeral! Those previously farmed oysters in Jointer Creek were large, oval, single specimens. BS popped open one of the oysters with a homemade metal oyster knife and slurped it right out of the shell and exclaimed, "Damn, that is the best oyster I have had today—salty and delicious!" He gave one to Wilder to eat, and he agreed they were the best he had ever eaten. A bushel was harvested in less than thirty minutes, and BS remarked that they had just saved $60—that is what a "fat sack" would sell for at the seafood market. The first step to prepare the oyster feast was using a pressure washer to blast off any mud as they were emptied out on the wooden dock. The plan was to steam most of them and use the rest for a wonderful stew consisting of oysters, milk, butter, salt, and pepper. The buzzards started circling as the oysters were cooking—that was the name given to the guys who always showed up when the food was cooking at the marina. It didn't take long for the oysters to start opening on the tin placed over the fire and covered by a wet croker sack. Catfish showed up with a large mason jar full of moonshine that had a peach inside for added flavor. He said a cousin from North Carolina had made it and brung him some cause he liked him. BS took a long pull of the shine and told the group, "This is quality white lightning!" Wilder tasted the shine and almost fainted and decided to stick with his beer.

During the eating and drinking, Wilder asked the group what they thought about his recently developed plan to have a dolphin sightseeing tour business as well as a charter-fishing business focusing on Cumberland Island. He could use his knowledge of the island that he was learning from BS to entertain and inform his clients. He figured that if those cats in Savannah could make money from tourists, then the sky was the limit for him. Catfish volunteered to be the bartender on the dolphin tours and serve moonshine which was quickly voted down. Everyone encouraged him to go for it and gave him some ideas such as including charter trips that specialize in catching sharks. The St. Andrews sound in front of Cumberland was purported to be one of the largest shark breeding areas on the coast, and why not let those tourists have an adventure catching "Jaws!"

Wilder estimated he had eaten fifty-plus steamed oysters, and he decided to take his oyster stew home in a large Styrofoam cup to eat later. He would ask BS to help him develop a business plan the next day while working at the marina and learning more about the history of the island from the master teacher.

The names Thomas Morrison Carnegie and Lucy Coleman Carnegie were written on the flip chart, and BS told Wilder these two people influenced how Cumberland was to become what it is today. He also said that today's lesson might be abbreviated because he had the "runs" from drinking that white lightning the night before. He began by stating ole Tom had accumulated a pile of money and used $35,000 to buy 4,000 acres on the island, including Dungeness, and paid $40,000 to buy 8,240 acres from Robert Stafford. Dungeness was rebuilt after it burned in

1885, and this mansion with a granite face would cost over $4.5 million in today's dollars. Tom only enjoyed the mansion for a short time because he died of pneumonia at age forty-three, a year after it was completed. His wife Lucy now became the indisputable matriarch of Cumberland. She knew her fortune was due to her husband Tom and his brother Andrew who started out in poverty and rose to immense wealth and power. Lucy Coleman Carnegie (as in Coleman camping gear) bought more real estate after Tom died to include the Stafford land with its mansions. She would later give the Stafford estate to William Coleman Carnegie and his wife Martha Gertrude Ely in 1887.

In January 1907, Lucy was served a subpoena stating two women, Cornelia Stafford Williams and Nancy "Nanette" Stafford Gassmann, claimed they were the offspring of Robert Stafford and a slave named Catherine. They claimed they were the rightful heirs to 7,700 acres that once belonged to Stafford but was now in Lucy's name. They lost the suit, enabling Lucy to bestow her land and fortune to her own children. Lucy said that she had always wanted to die on her beloved island, but after being treated for pneumonia, she died in Massachusetts. She did get one last wish—she was buried in Cumberland in the family cemetery.

The Great Depression had its impact on all America, including Cumberland Island. In 1925, Andrew II and his wife Bertha boarded up the Dungeness mansion and moved to the less opulent Stafford estate. During this time, some of the Carnegie descendants decided to make some much-needed money and would get into the restaurant business in Camden County, Georgia. Morris and Virginia Carnegie had two sons, Tom and Carter. Tom attended Harvard and played baseball and football and was offered a major league baseball tryout. When he failed to make it, he decided to open up a restaurant and lounge in the early 1930s along with some tourist cabins on Highway 17 before I-95 was built. The complex was named Tomochichi, and much of the formal dining room furniture of Dungeness was moved there. Liquor was sold there, and Saturday night dances were popular. (Georgia was dry at this time, but the local law enforcement allowed it to happen.) Tom also built a zoo next to the cabins and had cages with some of the animals from Cumberland, including alligators, black bears, and a bald eagle. The restaurant served the finest of foods often cooked by Blacks, but other Blacks still had to order from a window located on the side of the building since they were forbidden to be inside like other customers. Blacks had a major influence on Cumberland, and in 1893, the first African church was built. At this church in 1993, John Kennedy Jr. and Carolyn Bessette were married. Back in 1890, the Half Moon Bluff tract was divided into fifty-two lots, 50 × 100 feet, and many former Black slaves purchased these lots.

A magnificent mansion called Plum Orchard was constructed for Lucy's son George Lauder Carnegie and wife Margaret Thaw by the architectural firm Peabody and Stearns of Boston. Margaret was the sister of the notorious Harry Shaw, who in 1906 shot the famous architect Stafford White because of an affair with Shaw's wife. He was let out of jail because he was thought to be crazy and visited Plum Orchard, but most people shied away from him because of his unpredictable behavior and his wild eyes. The mansion had an enclosed swimming pool that was enjoyed by all the nieces and nephews. Margaret and George raised diamond-backed turtles and made a stew with cream and sherry that was so widely eaten that these turtles were almost driven to extinction. They had a pen in the marsh so salt water could come in the pen, and the turtles would lay their eggs on the part of the pen on the bank. There were also fifteen large horse stalls in a magnificent stable and a huge room for carriages, buggies, and carts.

In 1900, Greyfield House construction began for Lucy's daughter Margaret "Reta" Carnegie and husband Oliver Garrison Ricketson. The other mansion, Dungeness, was in its prime during this time. Lucy Carnegie owned 90 percent of the island until she died in 1915 with her will mandating none of the lands she passed on to her children to be sold while any of the children were alive. In 1930, Howard Candler Sr. and son purchased Cumberland Island property at High Point and later sold it to the Park Service for $9.6 million. They also made a deal of the century in 1982 by having the Park Service give them five years to rebuild or update any house or any structure they owned at High Point. In the agreement, the Candlers obtained retained rights on 38 acres until the death of the youngest shareholder, which will last well into the twenty-first century.

Other interesting dates that are part of Cumberland Island history were as follows: in 1955, Cumberland Island was named second to Cape Cod by the US National Park Service as places of national significance along the Atlantic and Gulf coast; in 1959, Dungeness mansion was set fire, and the Dungeness yacht also burned as a result of arson (the culprit was believed to be a deer poacher who had been shot and wounded by the overseer at Dungeness).

The two Dungeness mansions burned almost a hundred years—apart—could it have been haunted because it was built over a shell mound (possible burial site left by the Timucuan Indian tribe)? In 1962, the last of Lucy's children died, and some sold their land to various investors, including Charles Fraser, who owned one-fifth of the land on Cumberland Island. He wanted to develop this land like he did on Hilton Head, South Carolina, which he named Sea Pines.

He envisioned a resort and wilderness park, but his plans began to fall apart when the Carnegies learned about it and enlisted the help of the Park Service. They instructed their attorney from Atlanta, Thomas Morris, to draw up a bill that would be introduced in Congress to make Cumberland a national park. Some families on Cumberland were reluctant to sell their land to the Park Service, and they wanted a guarantee they would still have a home on the island, in retained lifetime estates, after the island became a national seashore. They also wanted in writing a promise not to develop the island and to never build a bridge to it.

In March 1970, the director of the National Park Service, George Hartzog, was contacted by billionaire Paul Mellon, chairman of the Andrew Mellon Foundation. At lunch on March 17, Hartzog was asked, "How would you like to own Cumberland Island?" The Park Service was eager to have Cumberland and prevent development there. Charles Fraser's property had to be acquired first, and the foundation would buy 75 percent of the island from the Carnegie descendants. Fraser was not a willing seller, but he was facing some serious financial problems at that time. Representative Bill Stuckey from Eastman, Georgia, introduced a bill in 1970 to make Cumberland a national seashore. The National Park Foundation, with a gift of $7.5 million from the Andrew Mellon Foundation, began the task of acquiring land from Charles Fraser and the Carnegies. The prices paid for the land, mostly Carnegie heirs, amounted to around $500 an acre. By the end of 1970, the foundation owned 75 percent of Cumberland. One stipulation of the Stuckey bill was that only structures built prior to 1970 could be repaired and inhabited. No new houses could be constructed as well as private structures. On October 23, 1972, Congress passed the bill designating Cumberland a national seashore to "preserve the historic and scenic character of the island." The Park Service eventually set a limit of three hundred people a day who could visit the island, and this number remained the same for those visitors who visit via ferry from St. Mary's, Georgia. In 1972, electricity was brought to the island from the mainland in anticipation of further development, which thankfully never happened!

BS concluded his history lesson by relating a couple of stories that keep the island in the national news. The first was Kings Bay Naval Base, which was behind Cumberland Island and was home to the nuclear submarine Trident—a 500-foot nuclear sub that carries twenty-four multiple-warhead missiles. Environmentalists had warned about the negative impact of dredging of the Cumberland River to accommodate these subs would have on the island. Another news item was the docks being built on some of the

1,000 acres of private land close to the National Seashore. In December 2016, Lunar LLC, a CI property owner, was granted a hardship variance by the Camden County Planning Commission to divide the 87.51 acres of their land into ten parcels formerly owned by the Rockefellers. Some feared new homes would be built, and they pointed out that it would be similar to seeing new homes being built in the Grand Canyon or Yosemite Valley—each crown jewels of National Park Service to which Cumberland Island belongs. One of the currently most bitterly contested developments was Space-X that would be built on Floyd's Creek facing Cumberland Island and only a few miles from the island. Rockets would fly over Cumberland Island and land in the Atlantic Ocean on the eastern side of the island. Folks were outraged at the impact a failed rocket mission would have on Cumberland Island.

CHAPTER 2

Meeting Maggie

Wilder began making more and more trips to Cumberland Island, taking charter groups to fish, conducting dolphin tours with history segments about the island, or going with Mark to explore. One day on a solo trip, he introduced himself to a lady who rode up on a four-wheeler and asked him what he was doing walking on Cumberland Island. His first impulse was to say, "None of your business. Who do you think you are, the queen of Cumberland Island?" but he had done his research via BS, so he used his charm and good looks and said, "I'm just a fisherman and environmentalist who is looking for ways to keep Cumberland Island just the way it is instead of proposed developments like the Lunar Corporation has planned." He had actually said the former to a ghost white Yankee wearing sandals with socks up to his knees when he asked him who gave him permission to throw his cast net in a tidal pool in Christmas Creek. Maggie and Wilder had an instantaneously solid friendship and began chatting about their concerns for the future of Cumberland Island. They walked to his boat, and she asked if he would mind taking her for a ride, and she would reciprocate by riding him to some neat places on the island on her four-wheeler. She wanted to go to the back of Christmas Creek and see if you could still exit the creek from there into the Cumberland River. She would later take him on a ride down to the Lake Whitney area to check on some turtle nests. A deal was made, and both saw a definite "win-win" situation.

Maggie was impressed with the new twenty-four-foot Sea Pro boat with a 300 hp Suzuki motor and all the electronics money could buy. Nice additions were the T-top with radar on it and a GPS trolling motor that kept the boat in position when the anchor button was pushed on the remote control. Maggie noted that the last boat she had been in was a fourteen-foot aluminum boat with a 9.9 hp that cranked sometimes, and often oars had to be used to move around in Christmas Creek. As they began the tour, she talked nonstop about Christmas Creek and how it had changed over the years. She asked if she could fish for a few minutes, and before the boat got anchored, she picked up a Penn 3000 spinning outfit, put a live mullet on it, and had it in the creek waiting for a bite. She hoped to catch a big flounder that she could bake with crab meat and Vidalia onions. Two minutes later, she was shouting, "Get the net! I've got the mother lode coming to the boat!"

A five-pound flounder was netted, and she started dancing around the boat, singing, "Maggie is a flounder pounder. Yeah, Yeah!" Not to be outdone, as soon as her fish was in the Yeti cooler, Wilder put a live shrimp on the business end of his Ambassadeur 5500C with a cork rig and floated it behind the boat, and *bam*, the cork disappeared, and he set the hook on a nice three-pound speckled trout.

After five more fish were caught, the captain turned off the trolling motor and fired up the 300 hp Suzuki to go to the back of the creek to explore the three forks located there.

As they eased along the bank, a herd of horses appeared on the left side, where a long stretch of oyster shells lined the bank. Maggie wanted to look at the horses and said she recognized one of the mares that appeared to be in very poor health. She said the male horses were often healthier because of the toll the females took when giving birth to their young. Her face was flushed, and her eyes teared up as she got on her soapbox about the travesty of allowing a non-native species to be subjected to such a terrible life on a place they did not belong.

She began her mini-lecture about horse history as Wilder thought to himself that this lady knew island history and could surpass even the master BS on her expertise. She said as far back as the 1780s, horses had been stocked on the island by early owners, and the population was estimated to be at two to three hundred. Most of the horses were unattended, but slaves had horses, and they were cared for since they were used for work and transportation. The Carnegies bought a train carload of Mustangs in 1921 from Globe, Arizona, and released them. These feral animals became the foundation of the present-day herds. Horses on Cumberland today have thousands of ticks, suffer from snakebites, have weak leg bones because of poor nutrition, and their guts are full of parasites. Many have drowned after being stuck in the marsh mud since they are not genetically salt marsh animals. Wilder decided to speed up the boat to let Maggie relax and catch her breath.

Fork #1, on the left, started producing some docks and houses that were built by some of the wealthy families who kept their land and did not sell to the National Park Service. Fork #2 also had some houses and docks, but Wilder was most interested in Fork #3. This was rumored to be the back way in and out of Christmas Creek, and it supposedly emptied into the Cumberland River. Maggie said she had done this before in a small boat on a high tide, and this gave Wilder the needed incentive to keep going even though the depth finder was flashing two feet, and the alarm was sounding. Five minutes later, this ill-defined creek dumped into the Cumberland River, so they knew they had made it. They turned around to go back to the main run of the creek. This would be valuable to know if you started out of the creek, and the wind had picked up or changed to the northeast, which could make for a dangerous situation in six- to eight-foot waves. Wilder had indeed cracked the hull of his fifteen-foot aluminum Bass Tracker boat several years ago, leaving the creek in rough seas. He was glad this type of boat had the entire bottom and sides filled with insulation, or it would have sunk!

After the water excursion, the two hopped on the four-wheeler and zoomed it down the beach without seeing anyone for miles and finally stopped near Lake Whitney to examine some turtle nests, which had been flagged with yellow tape. This lake was the biggest freshwater lake on the island and had some of the highest sand dunes of any of the barrier islands. They checked to make sure the nests were intact and then raced back to the boat where before departing, she gave him her cell number, and he gave her his business card with all his contact info on it. She cautioned him that cell phone service was unpredictable on the island, and only about 50 percent of the island received and sent phone messages. They both agreed that if they really needed to talk, they would use channel 55 on their VHF radios, which both had. They waved goodbye, and Wilder knew he had made a friend that could help him learn secrets about the island nobody else knew, and maybe this was another "ace in the hole!"

Three days later, Wilder's cell phone rang, and Maggie invited him to come visit her at her cabin and take a look at her museum. She promised him an exotic meal he would never forget and asked him if he liked his margaritas frozen like she preferred. She told him she had some nice pinot noir wine she had made from the small grapes she grew, which was light in color and had a taste resembling black-berries. He said he was in and volunteered to bring some Italian bread and cheese from Publix. She had made some arrangements for him to leave his boat at the Park Service's dock and told him she would pick him up on a wild horse bareback and give him a ride to her cabin. She actually showed up on her four-wheeler and had fun playing the joke on him. She looked radiant in her freshly washed cut-off denim overalls and a bright red UGA T-shirt. Wilder had on the usual fishing guide attire, long sleeve yellow Columbia fishing shirt, shorts, and some very ugly brown Crocs. She gave him a tour of the museum with hundreds of animal species she was dissecting on tables, and the walls were filled with horns and antlers, some of which he had never seen. She had hand-sized sharks' teeth and whale bones from a dead right whale that had washed up on the beach.

After the tour, they each sat in a homemade rocking chair on the front porch and enjoyed the sights and sounds of island life. The porch was decorated with nets, driftwood, and the yard had several rusting pieces of machinery and, of course, the proverbial old truck perched on four blocks without wheels. He laughed and said now he knew she was a redneck as she explained that an older gentleman had given that to her years ago because she kept him supplied with moonshine that she always had an ample supply of. She told him that the old 51 Ford truck with a flat head V-8 was a collector's item she planned to fix one day but could not find time in her busy schedule to work on it.

Nature was in full force as the two listened to an owl nearby making "who who" sounds and watched multicolored hummingbirds fight each other for some nectar she had put in a hanging mason jar. A bluebird arrived on the porch, followed by one of the most beautiful birds in existence—a blue-, green-, red-, and yellow-painted bunting. After a delicious frozen margarita, Maggie served her specialty, venison spaghetti, accompanied by her pinot noir. Both cleaned their plate, had another glass of wine, and both enjoyed one of the finest cigars money could buy—a Black and Mild bought by him at the Friendly Express store at an exorbitant price of ¢79 each.

CHAPTER 3

Meeting McKenzie at Greyfield Inn

Wilder began spending more and more time on Cumberland Island, where he became friends with some of the locals, did favors for the Park Service, and used his boat to get supplies to Greyfield Inn for the guests. One afternoon, he received a call from the head chef inviting him to spend a few days at the inn, free of charge as a gesture to repay him for all his help. He immediately agreed to come and looked forward to the splendid ambience he knew awaited him.

Wilder began to study and to learn the history of the houses built on Cumberland with most of his expertise coming from his mentor, Captain BS, and by reading all the books he could find out about the island. Dungeness was the most unique home ever built there being it was the first four-story tabby home reported to be built in the United States. It was built in 1802 by the Englishman Phineas Miller. The tabby used was a conglomerate of shell and lime. It had three stories over a high basement and had an attic at the top. The kitchen was detached from the house because of summer heat, which was a common southern feature. It had walls 6 feet thick at the base narrowing slightly to 4 feet above the ground. It was built on top of a large shell mound, which could have placed it 76 feet above ground level. The land it was built on was high land approximately 20 feet above sea level, making the very top reach an incredible 96 feet above sea level. The house faced north on a terrace made of granite, and the upstairs floor had twenty rooms. There were four brick chimneys to each end wall and sixteen fireplaces. Magnolia and live oak trees surrounded the house, and its gardens had groves of orange, peach, and olive trees. The overall effect was tropical, and giant century plants, sago palms, and date palms abounded in the surroundings. The house had a covered observation platform on which visitors could view the harbor. It was reported the magnificent view from the top allowed visitors to see Amelia Island, the Atlantic Ocean, and the mainland.

Sometime after April 23, 1866, Dungeness caught fire and burned almost to the ground. Only the brick chimneys and the tabby walls remained. It would remain that way until November 17, 1881, when Tom Carnegie bought it from General Davis for $35,000. On February 26, 1884, the cornerstone of the "New Dungeness" was laid, and the blueprint revealed it would measure 120 feet ×56 feet and would be two stories high with an attic. A hundred-foot tower would be on its east end. The main entrance would be on the north side and just inside would be a 10 × 11-foot vestibule with a marble floor that led in a twenty-one-foot wide grand hall. The parlor would be on the east side of the grand hall with the measurements of 18 × 24 feet. Other rooms included an 18 × 24-foot dining room, a gun room with a lavatory, and a master bedroom with its own bath. The second floor had guest bedrooms, the family's living apartments, a library with reading rooms, and six more bedrooms in the attic. The total cost of constructing and furnishing the home was estimated to be $285,000.

Upon completion, visitors would marvel at the workmanship of the house. Stained glass windows had been filled with flowers, fruit, and foliage surrounded by Japanese ornamentation. Also in the design was a large Scottish thistle. This beautiful flower had sharp thorns and was known to have a stubborn and tenacious grip on the dirt it was planted in—the defiant ability to flourish in spite of efforts to remove it. It stood for resiliency—a trademark of the Carnegie family.

At the top of the tower, visitors could enjoy panoramic views of the Atlantic Ocean pounding on the beach, the Cumberland River winding north, and Fernandina Harbor. At the bottom was the basement housing the servant's apartments that had hot and cold running water. Gas manufactured on the premise powered a hot-air system for heating the house, a system for ringing bells to summon servants, and electric lights. In 1885, Lucy Carnegie wrote that the new house would be furnished and would have a refrigerator, sewing machine, telephone rentals, and an American flag.

All things must come to an end. After World War II ended and the military left Cumberland, postwar inflation and high labor costs made keeping up Dungeness impossible. Roads became impassable, docks rotted, and other buildings caved in because of neglect. The gardens were now full of weeds. The beautiful fountain quit flowing, and the walkways cracked and crumbled. The second Dungeness's final hour occurred after sunset on June 24, 1959. As it was burning, the bright orange flame could be seen all the way to Brunswick, Georgia, which was over 20 miles away. One theory was the fire was started by a disgruntled poacher, wounded by a caretaker a few weeks earlier who sneaked back on the island and set fire to it for revenge.

Wilder was also curious about the place he would be visiting soon, Greyfield Inn. Captain BS told him Mama Carnegie had it built in 1901 for Retta and Oliver Ricketson. Retta was the oldest daughter of Lucy and Tom Carnegie. It was about 2 miles north of Dungeness, and this three-story stucco mansion overlooked a high bluff on Cumberland Sound. The Ricketsons spent only the winters there and brought Lucy and her older brother Ollie there where they were privately tutored in the schoolroom, which had been built and was connected to the pergola—open with a lattice roof.

Oliver and Retta separated before Lucy was a teenager, and she later married Bob Fergueson, whose family was in the lumber business in New Bedford, Connecticut, and whose grandfather had quarried granite at Mount Desert Island in Maine. The couple was given the use of Greyfield through an arrangement with the trustees of Maria Carnegie's trust. Retta and Bob had four children—Bobby, Retta, Ricky, and Cindy.

In 1964, with no money coming in to take care of the mansion and other buildings, Lucy and Bob realized they could no longer afford Greyfield and its upkeep. They devised a plan with the help of their son Rick to turn Greyfield into an inn. They renovated the old mansion and closed in some old porches to make more bedrooms. The inn opened in 1965, and Rick and his wife Edith were chosen to run it. Lucy was actually the person who ran the place, bossing people around, making rules for all to abide by. It became a power struggle between Rick and Lucy because she thought of herself as the "queen" of Greyfield. She fired Rick and hired a new manager named John Frank Fox IV, an experienced hotelier, who she later fired.

Wilder looked forward to his visit to one of the most exclusive inns in America. The price to stay there was much higher than his budget would allow ($775 per night), but his stay would be free. The inn was owned by Miss Lucy's descendants under the name of Greyfield Limited Partnership. Wilder would need to get a new jacket to wear because he knew Miss Lucy would still be requiring gentlemen to wear jackets at dinner—at least he would not be required to wear a tux! Finally, the day of his trip arrived. He was allowed to dock his boat at the ferry dock, and he was taken to the inn by one of the men who worked there. He was amazed at the elegance of the inn and its persona. He had visited several nice hotels while in college while attending conferences, such as the Biltmore in Asheville, North Carolina, and the Peabody in Nashville, Tennessee. Both were nice, but neither possessed the southern charm of this mansion that looked like it could have been in the book *Gone with the Wind*.

One plan Wilder had on his agenda was to explore places on the island he had learned about but never had visited. He wanted to explore the lighthouse on the northern end and the ruins of Dungeness on the south end and see for himself the colossal hundred-foot sand dune facing the beach. Since his history lessons showed two-forts built on the island, he wanted to spend several hours searching for artifacts in hopes of finding items, such as buttons and coins. Would he find a treasure at some of these places? Maybe, maybe not.

He was assigned to the bedroom called Stafford suite, and he unpacked his suitcase and decided to change into some nicer clothes since he wanted to make a nice first impression on the owner and other guests. He looked at himself in the floor-length mirror and thought that his new light-blue seer suckle suit made him look like he belonged in "GQ." His white polo shirt went well with the suit, and his last item was a pair of alligator loafers and, of course, no socks! He knew it was time for cocktail hour, and after introducing himself to several guests, he saw a lady who could have been the movie star Natalie Woods's twin. She introduced herself as McKenzie but told him to call her Mac for short. He remembered from his history lesson that she was the fifth innkeeper of Greyfield and a descendant of the Carnegie family. She led him to a massive oak bar, and he ordered his favorite top-shelf cocktail, a gray goose martini, straight up with extra olives. She ordered an A. H. Hirsch Reserve bourbon that was very smooth and cost a mere $2,892 a bottle. They seemed to lock eyes, and both felt that they were the only ones in the room. After a few minutes, the dinner bell was rung, and Mac insisted her new friend sit next to her during dinner. He readily agreed and asked her what the main course would be, and she said her guests were treated with the inn's specialty the first night, "armadillo on the half shell."

The armadillo turned out to be the "catch of the day," which was crab-stuffed flounder, but first, they had to endure a freshly caught shrimp cocktail and she crab soup with the crabs caught that day from the ferry docks. He was not a connoisseur of fine wine, and he asked her to choose a nice white wine for both of them to have with the seafood. She ordered her favorite, which was Santa Margarita, a pinot grecio, which was made and bottled in Italy. The dinner was indeed a five-star feast of perfection, and nobody could refuse the blackberry cobbler topped with homemade vanilla ice cream. After dinner, the guests gathered on the front porch to chat and, of course, drink some more poison of their choice. Wilder decided to go with a Bud Light because he knew if he kept drinking the hard stuff, he would say something stupid. He engaged in conversation with an older gentleman who hailed from South Rockland, Maine, who introduced himself as Captain Jim Smart. The captain was smoking a brierwood pipe filled with some type of tobacco, which he later learned was called Lane's Limited Blend I-Q. He felt silly lighting up his seventy-nine-cent Black and Mild cigar, but that's what he liked once a day, and so be it. The captain said he was retired from a life on the high seas and now was the chief liar and yarn spinner at the Sail, Power, and Steam Museum of South Rockland, Maine. He stated that as a young man, he had polio but had been taught by his rugged father how to make lemonade when life gives you a bag of lemons. As a small boy, he had always "went down to the boat" with his father and began his adventure from Coastal New England to European canals to the high seas.

He had owned thirty-five different ships/boats in his lifetime, and one of his favorites was the "Adventure," a 122-foot × 25-foot wooden Grand Banks fishing schooner, which was a pure sail vessel, 6,000 sq. ft., 230 tons. It was a thirty-seven-passenger, seven-crew, Maine coast vessel built in 1926 that was retired from the windjammer fleet in 1988. He currently only had two boats, which consisted of a forty-seven-foot fiberglass Kenner powered by a gas Volvo engine and named "Funky Old Thang," and his "haul ass" boat named "Spodie Odie," which was a twenty-six-foot twin-screw Powercat with twin 135 Evinrudes. Wilder described his new boat, and the captain joked that it seemed like those southern boys had more horsepower than sense! He told Wilder he and his wife had planned a trip south and were planning to stay at a B&B on Amelia Island, Florida, but she found Cumberland while doing her research, and their decision was a no-brainer. Wilder, who always liked to make deals, told captain that he would show him Cumberland Island via his boat if he promised to show him around Penobscot Bay when and if he ever made it to Maine.

They shook hands, exchanged business cards, and saw the captain's wife and Mac chatting while enjoying their drinks. Introductions were made, and Wilder found out that Meg, Captain's wife, was as interesting as her husband and told the group that she was the "brains behind their museum—all Jim does is talk and spins yarns if he had an audience who will listen to him!" The foursome talked about the differences between Maine and Georgia, and Wilder was interested to learn Mac had actually been to Maine on a small cruise line that only carried one hundred passengers. She said her adventure began when she flew into Portland, Maine, and boarded the ship named "Independence" for seven days of learning about the bays and ports. She said she went to Bar Harbor, Acadia National Park, Camden, Castile, Belfast, Rockland, and her personal favorite Booth Bay Harbor. Mac enjoyed taking pictures of lighthouses and told the group that Maine was the nation's lighthouse capital. Wilder thought this trip was now on his "bucket list" as the couples departed from each other with plans to reconnect soon.

Wilder wanted to know everything about Mac, and when asked, she told him she had gone to school in Providence, Rhode Island, and attended art school in Massachusetts. She moved to Cumberland in 1978 after a divorce and began designing jewelry from shells and bones she found on the beach and inland areas. He was surprised when she told him that Greyfield Inn was built for her grandmother, Margaret Carnegie, and became an inn run by her brother Rick who opened it in 1965. She showed him some of the pieces she designed, and she told him she used a process called "lost wax casting," which involves filling a mold with gold or silver. Prices for her pieces started at $55, and some had sold for $12,000. Her studio she led him into had turtle shells, alligator external bone plates, seashells, dolphin vertebra, and shark teeth. She said one of her most famous designs were the wedding bands she designed for John F. Kennedy Jr. and Carolyn Bessette, which were snake ribs cast in gold. They were married in the First African Baptist Church on Cumberland, September 21, 1996. Their lives ended in a plane crash in July 1999.

Mac explained that she had gotten her love of nature from her grandmother Lucy Ferguson who had been the quintessential adventurer, and the story was told about the time she had used her buck knife to kill a large rattlesnake, which had invaded her chicken coop. She taught Mac how to skin a rattlesnake and mount it on a piece of driftwood, ride wild horses, hike, and to recognize the footprints of various animals. A favorite trip was to go to the beach and watch loggerhead turtles lay their eggs and later watch the newly hatched small turtles make the long, dangerous journey to the Atlantic Ocean.

Plans were made for a beach trip the next day to watch the eastern sunrise and to search for shells and other sea presents that had washed up on the beach during the night. The sunrise was extraordinary and lit up the horizon with bright orange color as it rose, looking like a giant bubble. Shells and sea creatures—some dead and some alive—covered the beach, and a large canvas bag was filled in two hours. Next, they rode to Dungeness to check out the giant old burnt mansion and examine the bricks that made up the giant chimneys. On the way to their next stop, they saw a herd of wild horses near the giant sand dunes of Lake Whitney. The lake itself was full of animals, including an alligator that looked to be at least 12 feet long. They took a few pictures with their phones, and since it was close to lunchtime, they went back to the inn for a picnic under the canopy of a 150-year-old live oak tree. Shrimp salad was loaded on a hoagie bun, assorted fruit of watermelon, pineapple, blueberries, and cold sweet tea were enjoyed by all the guests except the captain and his wife. Where could they be?

After lunch, they decided to take a scenic tour of the island in Wilder's boat he had left docked beside the Cumberland Queen. Mac wanted to go to the jetty rocks located on the southern tip of the island, and they loaded up and headed south. On the way, Mac noted the huge facility, which was Kings Bay Naval Station, located on the western side of Cumberland. She told Wilder that most of the island's residents opposed it because to acquire enough depth for the huge nuclear submarines stationed there, the river had to be dredged. The theory was this deepening would negatively impact all the creeks on the western side of the island. The Navy had already dredged one creek that had become much shallower after the dredging of the main river.

They decided to ride into Beach Creek on their way to the jetties to see the huge sand dune at the end of the creek. This dune stood out from all the rest because of its extreme height, and visitors enjoyed tumbling down this high, soft dune and land on the beach. Mac told the story of finding two naked sunbathers at the bottom of this dune as she and a friend used their boogie boards to take the wild ride down. She figured these northern folks were truly nudists because they never covered up but just smiled and said hello. Wilder remarked that maybe they could go back and could get a glimpse, but Mac shook her head and told him it was not a pretty sight to behold. They motored out of the creek, and after rounding the southern tip of the island, they were at the jetties.

A discussion was held regarding who, how, and when these and the other jetties jutting out from the northern tip of Amelia Island, Florida, happened—a topic to research later. As they slowly entered the area close to the beach called Pelican Banks, they spotted a giant manatee with a device attached to the top of its head, moving slowly away from the beach. Mac conveyed that the Department of Natural Resources did that to track these magnificent, prehistoric animals to learn their migration habits. She added that Florida had many more manatees than Georgia because of warmer water temperatures and the springs located all over the "gator nation." They eased out to the end of the rocks where the water was clear and a sea-green color. Fish were feeding and knocking bait out of the water in a wild frenzy. Always ready like a competent captain should be, he cast a large surface plug toward the school, handed the rod and reel to Mac, and watched the action begin. A fifteen-pound bluefish inhaled the lure, and as the drag sang, Mac was pumping the rod and squealing with delight. They kept two of these badass fish as the captain described how delicious they were when cooked on a smoker for a couple of hours. He explained why he called them "badass" because he had seen a fishing buddy of his bitten by one while trying to remove the hook from its very toothy mouth.

As they headed north, they passed Stafford Beach, Lake Whitney's high bluffs, Christmas Creek, and the lighthouse. After rounding the tip and heading south, they motored into Brickhill River and decided they needed to have another adventure like this very soon.

CHAPTER 4

The Island—Its Rich History

Wilder had now met two of the most influential women ever to set foot on Cumberland Island. He had read several books loaned to him by BS, and now he was ready to explore and learn more about the island that seemed to captivate him. He learned that Cumberland was the largest of Georgia's barrier islands, which included Jekyll, Saint Simons, Ossabaw, Sappelo, and Saint Catherine's. These unique landforms acted as a layer between the ocean and the mainland. They were separated from the shore by a bay or sound and protected the coast from being impacted by storm waves or high winds. The side that faces the ocean often had beautiful undisturbed beaches and large sand dunes. The western side had salt marshes and barrier flats which were closer to the mainland. These areas were home to a wide variety of wildlife and plants. These islands were constantly changing because of storms, waves, wind, and sea-level changes. Waves and storms could erode sand dunes, and strong currents could move sand from one end of the island to the other. Most captains who fished

Cumberland find this out every year when they found out the route to Christmas Creek had shifted 200 to 300 yards.

Cumberland Island was comprised of 36,000 acres and was one-third larger than Manhattan. It was 18 miles long and ranged from one to half to three miles in width. Its beach had mixed flocks of shorebirds, including sandpipers, gulls, terns, willets, oystercatchers, plover, and an endangered species, the piping plover. The tide swept numerous creatures to the beach, and that was where Maggie and Mac found most of their treasures. As the tide receded, starfish, jellyfish, horseshoe crabs, snails, blue crabs, and a variety of small fish such as mullet were trapped in small tidal pools and were easy prey for birds and humans. Sea fans and sand dollars were a favorite for beachcombers to find and admire. One interesting crab was the ghost crab, which got their name because of their pasty white color and the ability to vanish in the blink of an eye. Wilder once threw one into the tent occupied by a friend, and havoc was instantly created.

Young sand dunes were the island's first defense against the sea. Deep-rooted plants such as sea oats anchored the dunes, keeping them stabilized. Further back, taller dunes rising higher than 50 feet protected the island from winds and storms. Often lakes were behind the dunes such as the largest lake on Cumberland, Lake Whitney, which had partially been filled in with sand. It still produced excellent fishing with its sapphire blue water and numerous aquatic weeds. It was home to alligators and long-legged egrets, herons, and ducks that arrived in the winter. Next inward were the maritime forests consisting of live oaks, water oaks, pines, palmettos, laurel oaks, southern magnolias, red bays, and sweetgums.

Many of the live oak trees on Cumberland were among the largest in America and were indeed the true southern tree and reminded one of *Gone with the Wind* scenes with Spanish moss hanging from the giant limbs down to the ground. These trees took on a majestic persona with massive trunks sometimes 8 feet in diameter and limbs that spread 40-plus feet. These limbs often sank to the ground and made a great place to sit for a scenic photo. The live oak was ideal for building tall ships because of its resistance to rot and insects. Because of its toughness and resistance, ships made of this wood could be hit by a cannonball and just bounce off. Men who were called "live oakers" came in the 1700s from Maine, Massachusetts, Connecticut, and New York in search of live oak trees on Cumberland. Timber was cut and hauled to shipyards in New England. This was the state tree of Georgia and was believed to live 300-plus years.

Next inland was the salt marsh near the rivers where it was bright green in the summer months and then became a glowing gold in the cooler months. This made for a breathtaking sight and was the reason why the coast of Georgia is called the "Golden Isles." The marsh and mud had a distinct smell, and locals who lived close to it often remarked that it was a pleasant smell to them, but visitors often said it had a rank, unpleasant smell. The marsh was one of the most biologically productive systems on earth, more fertile than the rich farmlands found in the West. Experts agreed that an acre of salt marsh might produce 5 to 10 tons of organic matter, while most fertile farms could produce only half that much. When the marsh grass died, it decomposed into a protein-rich waste. It supported oysters, clams, shrimp, pogies, croakers, and squid. One square acre of marsh could support a million fiddler crabs that eat dead fish or plants. Cumberland's salt marsh nourished an estimated 70 percent of all commercially important fish and shell-fish. Raccoons, otters, minks, and armadillos roamed the marsh looking for an easy dinner. Christmas Creek curved through the marsh on the northern tip of Cumberland between big and little Cumberland. It emptied into the Atlantic Ocean on an outgoing tide, and an incoming nutrient-rich (and fish-rich) water covered the oyster shells and marsh grass. BS swore Christmas Creek got its name because it always produced gifts—fish, shrimp, clams, or oysters. He was quick to add, "Three-fourths of the earth's surface is water, and one-fourth is land. Pretty clear that the good Lord intended man triple the time fishing and being on water than in the yard working in the dirt!"

Since man had a tendency to want to mess with nature, he did so with the Cumberland River in 1939. Congress ordered that the river, which is part of the Intracoastal Waterway, be deepened to a uniform depth of 12 feet at mean low water. In 1890, it was 5.5 feet at mean low water, and this resulted in treacherous navigation for most boats.

In 1881, another man-made project was undertaken, which was the construction of the rock jetties from the southern tip of Cumberland Island out into the ocean. This was the entrance channel to the Saint Mary's River and produced many changes in the local shoreline and the southern Cumberland dune system. The jetties altered tidal flow, coupled with a predominantly southern longshore current, caused an increase in sand and the establishment of a valuable dune system.

In 1887, artesian wells were drilled on the island, and these tapped into the underground freshwater river known as the Florida aquifer. It was under immense pressure and, when tapped, produced a free-flowing "artesian" water supply. This produced the fresh water necessary for survival, and early settlers used hydraulic pumps to pump well water in large wooden tanks. These were mounted on scaffolding and provided an unlimited supply of water for Greyfield, Dungeness, Plum Orchard, Stafford, and the hotel located on the north end of the island. If you have ever had the opportunity to drink this water, you will notice it is a cool, crisp, refreshing taste. Cattle, horses, and other animals used this water to drink to stay alive.

When asked who were the first known humans to reside on Cumberland, BS maintained the Timucuan Indians were there long before the white explorers made landfall. They lived on the island peacefully for centuries. They were handsome and tall, with some of the men over 7 feet tall and some women over 6 feet tall. They spoke a different language than their neighbors, the Guale Indians, who resided on islands to the north. They called Cumberland several different names, including Missoe (beautiful), Wissoe (sassafras), and Tacatacuru, meaning "beautiful island." Most of the men and some of the women covered their bodies with elaborate tattoos, and they accomplished this by slicing their dark skin and rubbing soot and ashes into the bleeding wounds. They killed the first three Spanish missionaries to arrive in 1567, but the Spanish eventually took over the island and brought the flu, measles, smallpox, and syphilis with them. Within ten years, the tribe was practically wiped out, but one survivor was a female chieftain named Donna Maria Melendez, who fought with the Spanish against the mainland Guale Indians. She was named princess of the island for her strength and courage.

In the early 1700s, nearly all remnants of Spanish influence had disappeared from Georgia's Golden Isles, and now it was Great Britain's turn. The founder of Savannah, Georgia, General James Oglethorpe, was known as a God-fearing moralist and a strict disciplinarian, set out to create a buffer between the Spanish in Florida and the citizens of Savannah. He first established the settlement he called Darien, and later, he established Fort Frederica on Saint Simons, Georgia. After studying the crude maps of the Georgia coast, he determined that the island called San Pedro would be an ideal island to build a fort. He wanted to have a fort he named Saint Andrews to serve as a way to block to Spanish when they arrived from Florida. This site is known as Terrapin Point today, and it forms a fifty-foot bluff with its location unsurpassed to view oncoming marine traffic. In June 1737, Oglethorpe received a commission as the "general and commander in chief of the forces in Georgia and South Carolina." In 1738, the general took up temporary quarters at Fort Andrews to personally supervise repairs to the fort. A second fort named Fort Prince William was built on the south end of the island and had high log walls that made it the stronger of two forts. It overlooked the St. Mary's inlet and had two eighteen-pound cannons mounted on swivels to be able to spin around and fire on approaching Spanish vessels. The general was eager to beat the Spanish and took the offensive by using sea forces from South Carolina to unsuccessfully launch an assault on Fort San Marcos in Saint Augustine, Florida. Sidenote—this fort is now a major tourist destination and has daily tours.

On July 7, 1744, a battle called the Battle of Bloody Marsh took place on St. Simons, and General Oglethorpe, with a little over seven hundred men, defeated the Spanish. This ended Spanish claims to all territories north of Florida, and it guaranteed English control of the coast down to the St. Johns River in Florida.

In the 1750s, the closest Cumberland had ever come to establishing a town was a short-lived settlement called Barriemackie (Gaelic for Mackay's Town.) It was a small village of huts to shelter soldiers at the site that later became Fort Saint Andrews. Approximately twenty-four families had well-constructed huts, which were described as small houses with roofs made of dried palmettos. Built close to Christmas Creek, it had disappeared by 1753, but in 1755, it was named as one of only three settlements on the extreme southern part of the US.

An Indian trader and Quaker named Edmund Grey had a group of men who were hunters, cattlemen, and boatmen follow him to Cumberland, and they became known as "Grey's Gang." They established a semipermanent settlement in 1757 and engaged in small trade with the Spanish and the Indians for eight to ten years. It also disappeared when most of the gang moved to Saint Mary's, Georgia, Amelia, and Talbot Islands in Florida searching for work.

In 1763, the English began to grant land on Cumberland, but the island continued to remain thinly inhabited. Most of the applicants for land were wealthy

Georgia and South Carolina citizens. Most came from a group of socially and politically important Georgia planters who wanted to acquire vast tracts of land for rice cultivation. Many of these socially elite knew one another and were often related.

On May 27, 1776, Cumberland Island met the American Revolution when British forces anchored their ships just northeast of Cumberland. The British used the island as a meeting point for their generals, especially on the southern end, so they could use the resources there, such as the fresh water found at Dungeness. In the end, colonial America won the war by receiving support from France, Spain, and the Netherlands. Georgia and South Carolina were most affected by the war, but all the colonies gained their independence from Great Britain. George Washington was instrumental in leading the Americans to victory in numerous battles.

The next major war to affect Cumberland was the war of 1812 fought between Great Britain and the United States on US soil near the Atlantic Ocean and the Gulf of Mexico. The US won again, and the Treaty of Ghent was signed on December 24, 1814. It began the "Era of Good Feelings," a period of national unity. Neither side lost territory, and a long-term effort was generally satisfactory for both sides, and both countries became close allies. Leading up to the end of the war, General Nathaniel Greene purchased land on Cumberland for timber harvesting to pay off his debts. After his death in 1786, his wife Catherine Greene inherited the property and became Catherine Greene Miller after marrying Phineas Miller. The family moved to the island in 1799 to grow Sea Island cotton and harvest the giant live oak trees. After his death, the Dungeness tabby was completed, and in 1803, a frequent visitor of Catherine's was none other than Eli Whitney, inventor of the cotton gin. She was rumored to have several prominent men vying for her attention, and she relished all this admiration.

"Cotton is king" is a favorite saying in South Georgia, and this "white snow" is seen growing in hundreds of fields in coastal counties. The Sea Island cotton grown on Cumberland grew well on the sandy, barren pine soil. The best and silkiest fibers were produced where moisture-laden sea breezes supposedly made the staple longer and glossier. The planters had a belief that the best cotton produced had ocean exposure. Seeds were planted in March, and in July, the plants began to blossom. Around August, the bolls began to open, and the field hands began the first of ten to twelve successive pickings, which continued to early January. The cotton was dried, and slaves sorted it by hand, separated the fiber from the seed, and cleaned the cotton of cracked seeds and foreign particles. It took great skills patience to grade the cotton, and this is why it was mostly done by women. The market value depended on the cleaning process before it was made into bales. Insects were a major problem, and rain and hail could kill the plants, but farmers often said the hard rains also helped kill the destructive caterpillars. The price of cotton varied in the marketplace, and often the cotton was stored until the market price rose. The cotton that was grown on St. Simons and Cumberland islands were some of the finest the world had ever seen.

Catherine Greene Miller died in 1814, and in her will, she left the Dungeness mansion to her daughter Louisa

Shaw. After Louise's death, her nephew Phineas Miller Nightingale inherited the mansion. He encountered financial trouble and sold various parts of his holdings to Robert Stafford Jr. Stafford became the largest plantation holder on the island, and it evolved into primarily plantations with numerous slaves. Because of his tremendous impact on Cumberland, let's devote some time to learn about this man.

CHAPTER 5

Robert Stafford—His Impact on Cumberland

Robert Stafford was born in 1790 on the south end of Cumberland. His father and uncle worked for General Greene and later for Caty and Phineas Miller. They supervised the construction of the Dungeness mansion as well as managing their cotton-growing operation and timber harvesting. When his father died in 1800, Robert remained on the island with his mother Lucy and two sisters. After her husband's death, she bought 125 acres of land on the island for $187 and later married Isham Spalding, a friend of her late husband who also owned land on the island.

Robert was very bright, and his mother arranged for him to attend a Yankee boarding school in New London, Connecticut, where he excelled. He became friends and established long-lasting relationships with very prosperous men such as Daniel Copp, a Connecticut ship owner who came to St. Mary's, Georgia, often and bought a plantation near the town. One of Copp's ships carried Robert to the

New London Grammar School, and he lived with his family in nearby Groton. Robert became lifelong friends with their son, Belton, who was six years younger than Robert. After finishing school in 1806, Robert returned to Georgia and became a private banker and obtained vast tracts of land by lending money to borrowers who put their land up as collateral. When several defaulted on their loans, he foreclosed and purchased their land, where he usually planted rice and cotton. He and his mother and sisters, in 1813, bought nearly 600 acres of land on Cumberland for $3,000. That land area is still known as Stafford Plantation today.

He purchased slaves to be used in rice cultivation and dreamed of owning all Cumberland. In 1839 and the 1840s, he foreclosed on many borrowers who he had loaned as much as $8,000 and often became the owner of their slaves and their land. He also acquired a five-hundred-acre tract known as Spring Plantation, which later was called Greyfield. Mr. Grey had put it up as security for a $3,500 loan, and when he died, his family could not cover his debt. In 1843 at a sheriff sale in Saint Mary's, for debt nonpayment, Phineas Nightingale was forced to sell his 4,200 acres on the island. Stafford had now accumulated 8125 acres, about one-third of greater Cumberland Island.

It seemed as though everything Robert touched turned to gold. He produced some of the finest cotton in the world, his Sea Island cotton, which often brought an astonishing ¢75 per pound. Factories in the US and England could not get enough of this fine product with strong fiber. Robert never married, and in the 1820s, he built his mother and sister, who were both widowed, a stately new plantation home—a large two-story pleasant framed dwelling. Mother and sister both became ill from yellow fever in 1836, and his good friend and nearest neighbor, Marguerite Bernadey, sent over her mulatto slave, Zabette, to help nurse them. She had lived at Plum Orchard, an impressive plantation located on Brickhill River, which got its name from the hundreds of wild plums growing there.

Marguerite was Zabette's grandmother, and when asked about going to live with Robert, her response was she hated to leave her grandmother, but since Mr. Robert had always been there to help them, she would go. He had indeed offered the family valuable financial advice and was always available to help take care of planting problems. Robert was willing to take Zabette on any terms her grandmother required since, in 1835, Georgia law made it illegal to free a slave; therefore, the law made it difficult for blacks to live in Georgia. In the end, her grandmother persuaded her that she was fortunate to have a gentleman like Mr. Robert to choose her for his companion.

She would oversee the cook named Amanda in cooking and cleaning, and she would be responsible for planning the meals since she was now formally leased from Marguerite. Although there was no formal ceremony, no wedding contract, and no guests, Robert told Zabette he had a vow that was his word. He proclaimed, "If not before a man of God then before God himself, till death do us part." Robert built a large tabby cottage next to his own house, and it was furnished nice and simple. He called it "Zabette's Cottage" to his white friends, but in reality, the only person living there was Amanda. Stafford was fifty-one years old when eighteen-year-old Zabette and two-year-old Mary were conveyed to him for $1. In essence, they were a gift.

Zabette had a deep love for the islands and everyone who lived there, especially the slaves who worked and often died there. She was a bright, studious young lady who originated the idea of building a hospital for the sick and also came up with a sketch and submitted it to Robert. He thought the plan was brilliant, and it was built and began immediately, helping patients mostly by Zabette, who had learned some folk remedies from her father.

Zabette had her and Robert's first child, a tiny light skin, beauty with black hair she named Mary Elizabeth. The baby changed Robert, who others viewed as haughty, silent, sour, with an almost constant frown. Now others saw a somewhat pleasant, almost handsome man who they enjoyed being around. Their next child was a boy they named Robert Stafford Jr., who everyone called Bobby.

Zabette's acceptance by others was difficult at times, especially by Phineas Nightingale and his wife. Phineas once confronted Robert a few days after the couples passed one another in their carriages, and Roberts smiled and tipped his hat to Miss Nightingale. When the two men next saw each other, Nightingale shouted, "Curse you, Stafford, don't ever greet my wife that way when you are with that mulatto whore and those bastard children!" He left quickly before Robert could get to the coward, but Robert had already begun to formulate several plans of revenge—perhaps a pistol duel, maybe a good old-fashioned ass whipping using bare fists, or the best idea of all, take away all his land that would ruin him and would be his downfall.

Option 3 was clearly the most intelligent choice and would give him the most pleasure.

Nightingale's demise began even without Robert's assistance. His financial problems had begun with the big freeze that happened in January 1835, where he lost practically all his orange trees. His crops were also ruined by the invasion in 1837 by the tiny insect called the purple mite. The final nail in the coffin was our country's worst depression, which devastated his assets. He had been saved from bankruptcy by relatives such as John Alsop King, then governor of New York. But sly Robert had an ace in the hole. Nightingale had not paid his taxes on his land for three years, and Robert bought his land at the courthouse steps. Robert had won again. He got his revenge and never had to fire a pistol or damage his knuckles!

Robert had a strong love for his children, taking a strong fatherly pride for them despite their mother being a slave. Under Georgia law, children born of a female slave were slaves themselves. The state legislature had denied a master's right to grant freedom to his slaves. That responsibility rested with the legislature. To protect his children, Robert decided to send them out of Georgia to New England, where they could live without enslavement. In violation of Georgia law, he had never registered them as slaves. He faced severe consequences if this was ever made public, and this concerned Robert because he had made some fierce enemies during several foreclosures. He sent his first three children—Mary, Robert, and Armand—to Connecticut to live with the Copp family and attend school there. Mary attended Baron Academy in Colchester, Connecticut, and the boys attended a small agricultural school. By 1852, two more daughters, Ellen and Adelaide Clarice, were born and later also sent to live with the Copps. Robert built an imposing home for all the children, and Zabette, a registered slave, would travel with Robert and stay with them in Groton. Their sixth child was born in 1853 and named Medora.

As a savvy investor, Robert began buying Connecticut properties such as office buildings, a farm, and a hotel, where he stayed during visits. He also invested in railroads and banks, and his friend Belton Copp managed his business affairs and set up trust for his children. He arranged their schooling and saw to their everyday needs. On her visits, Zabette was regarded as the children's live-in nurse and stayed with them during the duration of the Civil War.

Union soldiers overran the island in 1862, and most of the white families fled, but Stafford refused to leave. Slaves who had been taken to Amelia Island, Florida, by Union forces were granted passes to return to Cumberland. Some returned with guns and held Stafford hostage in his own home. On the foggy morning of September 1, 1862, Stafford sent an urgent message to the commander of the Union ship, the USS *Alabama*, asking for help. Union soldiers rounded the slaves up and locked them in the steamer's brig. It was believed the willingness of the Union commander to help a white southern plantation owner was because he had helped the Union army by providing supplies to them.

A forty-mile wide berth that stretched from Charleston, South Carolina, to Jacksonville, Florida called the "Sherman Reserve," was created by the military government when the war ended. The land within the reserve was seized by military decree, and its purpose was to redistribute the old plantation lands to the former slaves. Former plantation owners were eligible to get their land back under certain conditions. By 1867, Stafford's property, which included most of Cumberland Island, was restored to him, and he was back on the island once again.

In 1870, tax records showed Stafford owned 8,000 acres, a decrease of 125 acres, which was the result of the creation of the freedmen's settlements. After 1874, he reported that his total acreage was 8,125.

When the war ended, Zabette returned to Cumberland from Connecticut and found that during her absence, Stafford had taken up with another woman of Color, Catherine Williams, who had two daughters by him. Zabette retreated to the cottage next to the big house and lived as a housekeeper. Her daughters prospered in life, and Mary, the oldest, married a carpetbagger Republican in South Carolina's legislature. After they divorced, she married a Yale-educated doctor. The second daughter Ellen married a prominent artist and, after a divorce, married another artist. The youngest daughter Medora married a naval captain well known in New York's political circles. The fourth sister Addie moved to Paris and became a countess after marrying Count Charles Cybulski, a member of the Russian diplomatic corps. Robert and Zabette's sons did not have the same fortune as their sisters. The youngest Robert was mentally handicapped and died at age thirty. His brother Armand died of consumption at age twenty-one while serving as a Union Army soldier.

In his later years, Stafford was viewed as an eccentric old man who drank too much. He died in 1877 at the age of eighty-seven. His estimated fortune was $1,000,000 plus, and he left his money, bank and railroad stocks, property in Connecticut, and all other assets to his surviving daughters. The real estate he owned on Cumberland Island went mostly to his sister's children, who immediately put it up for sale. Zabette had been left out of the inheritance and moved to the north end of the island to live in a primitive hut. She lived long enough to see the Carnegies buy up the Stafford tracts of land and build their elaborate mansions on the south end. She lived ten more years after Robert passed away and died in obscurity in 1887.

CHAPTER 6

What's That Smell—Maybe Gold?

Every trip to the marina was always fun and entertaining for Wilder because he enjoyed hearing all the stories BS told, especially after a few beers. His stories often mentioned Cumberland, and many were so funny that he could not have made them up. The yarns really got hilarious when Catfish was there, and they competed to see who could get the most laughs. On a nice summer day that was so hot that the sand gnats were behaving and not trying to suck everyone's blood from their bodies, Catfish began the session. He started by asking BS if he remembered when his buddy, who was a preacher, put his boat in at the marina and had his wife's pretty little dog with him that resembled a small fox. Little Foxie liked to ride in the boat with the preacher and would often wait until the boat was hoisted in the water to jump in. That day, the preacher had forgotten his hat and went back to the truck and had not seen Foxie jump out of the boat when he got out. In typical fashion, he left the marina wide open but came roaring back in ten minutes frantically, exclaiming his little dog had blown out of the boat, and he needed help to find it. Catfish told the hysterical preacher to go look by the bait tank, and he would see a little sleeping dog. He had left Foxie and was relieved, knowing his wife would not be killing him for losing her dog!

BS began laughing when he asked Catfish if he remembered the other dog story involving the preacher. On this hot, summer day, the preacher had his family on the boat in their favorite spot on earth, Christmas Creek. He had followed his fishing buddy Captain Jim and his son to the creek, and the two boats anchored in the mouth to begin a day of fishing. The green ocean water was coming in, but the fish were not biting. John (the preacher) had his three children with him as well as his wife Dottie, and the kids wanted to get out to the boat and swim and fish from the bank. Captain Jim watched as the kids jumped out of the boat with their large German shepherd named Rocky, and each had a rod and reel baited with a live shrimp. As soon as the trio reached the sand, Rocky saw the flipping live shrimp dangling from the rod held by Betsy, the youngest daughter aged six, and jumped 3 feet in the air and inhaled it. The fun began—Rocky running down the beach with a hook lodged in his mouth and Betsy shouting for him to stop. Meanwhile, the preacher who had a speaker and a microphone, mounted on his console bellowed in his deep baritone voice, "Sit, Rocky, sit," over and over while everybody watched this comedy happen in real life. The line finally broke. The hook was removed from Rocky's mouth, but the memories never faded away.

BS had one more fishing story to share, and he began by telling the revival story. John had invited a visiting preacher who was preaching a revival and who was from

Alabama to go fishing before he preached the first service of the week. They did not have to be back at the church until six thirty that evening, so the plan was to put the boat in at St. Mary's, Georgia, and go to the Cumberland jetties for a day of fishing and fellowship. John had a reputation of having a lot of misfortune when he fished in salt water, but he never told that to Ernest, the revival preacher. It was rumored that the boat service called SeaTow knew him by his first name because they had rescued him so many times when he called them in distress. He also had a hobby of buying used boats and motors that would be dependable one day and quit working on another day.

On this day, John picked his finest rig with a relatively new motor to ensure the trip would happen with no setbacks, and they would be back in time for the church service. After a successful launch, the two preachers made it to the jetties and found the water to be somewhat muddy, and the fish did not bite very well. They had plans for an old-fashioned fish fry when they returned, but they needed a miracle with their catch of five fish. They stayed too long at the jetties but stopped at one more spot in the Saint Mary's River to put a few more fish in their cooler—didn't happen—and now they had to hurry to meet their deadline. The motor cranked but would not go forward when the throttle was moved forward. Somehow the propeller had fallen off the foot of the motor, and since they didn't see another soul, the plan was for John to get out of the boat and walk/crawl through the marsh in an attempt to make it to the main road to hitch a ride back to his truck and go looking for another prop. By the time he made it to the main road, John was covered in the black, gooey marsh mud, and he resembled the *Creature from the Black Lagoon*. After several men slowed, looked, and kept moving, one guy told him to jump in the back of his truck, and he would give him a ride. Another prop was located and put on the motor, and the two weary preachers made it to the church after a quick shower at 7:05 a.m.—only five minutes late while the hymn "Shall We Gather at the River" was being sung by the choir!

The beer was ice cold, and everyone was laughing when Catfish announced, "One mo story," before they roasted some oysters. He told the group about two of his favorite older gentlemen, Bert and Jim, who he found to be hilarious, but other fishermen never thought they were too funny. Bert owned the antique boat with a forty-year-old 75 hp Evinrude motor that was the size of a refrigerator. They liked to go to Cumberland to fish, especially in the summer months when the speckled trout were thick on the beach, and the whiting were abundant. Their trip would begin when they arrived at 5:00 a.m. at the marina, which opened for business at 6:00 a.m. They wanted to be first to put their boat in and to make sure they had live shrimp because they sometimes sold out fast. They also wanted to get to their favorite drop they called the "Whitaker Drop" before anyone else beat them there. These two gentlemen had one gear when they went fishing—"slow gear." They never had the boat loaded like most fishermen but instead had the bed of a vintage Chevy pickup loaded with batteries, coolers, rod/reels, life jackets, and an anchor Bert had crafted from a hundred-plus-pound farm plow. Everyone else had their boat ready, and all they had to do was get bait and ice. Bert also took an extra ten minutes to "top off" his portable gas tanks, and often others were calling them names and complaining about these "slow old farts!" One morning, a young, brash charter captain asked Bert why didn't he "get the lead out" instead of holding up the line, and his response was "Hey, little Snap-a-roo, maybe you should get your ass out of bed a little earlier so you could be first in line!" After a day of fishing, these two, especially Jim, were worn out and had back pain—probably from pulling in the hundred-plus pound plow anchor!

BS asked Wilder where his buddy Mark had been because he had not seen him in several days. Wilder explained that Mark had taken a job as a charter captain at the prestigious Cabin Bluff in Camden County and had a sweet deal. They furnished brand-new Pathfinder boats equipped with all the latest technology, new Penn rod/reels, lunches, plenty of beer, and live shrimp for bait. He could make good money, especially from tips from the rich boys who drank beer all day long. BS told Wilder he wanted to share his story of the "gold treasure" of Cumberland, but he would tell Wilder who could share it with Mark.

The gold was gold coins that had been hidden on Cumberland by a group of soldiers who had explored the island in the 1800s. There had been five coins recovered by treasure hunters since the island had been visited and inhabited by various groups from Spain, France, and England. Treasures of gold, silver, and jewelry had been discovered up the St. Mary's River, but no significant one had been found on Cumberland. Three different maps had weathered the years, and BS said he knew of two, but the third one was said to be in possession of the descendants of former slaves Primus and Amanda Mitchell.

Wilder asked BS if he could see the treasure maps and was told he would be shot if he told anyone other than Mark about them, and also, he would have to sign a contract that if he found, the treasure would be split up evenly three ways. Each one told of the ways they planned to spend their soon-to-be fortune, and BS said he would purchase a used fifty-four-foot cabin cruiser from a friend who had it for sale in Key West, Florida. He would then embark on his "dream trip," which would travel up the ICW from Florida to Canada. He knew this system of canals and rivers would provide ideal protection and allow for safety and comfort. He had already asked his friend Brandi, a bartender at the lodge on Sea Island, if she wanted to go with him, and her simple reply was "Hell yea." Even though she was thirty years younger, he knew she loved the water as much as she did and would be a pleasure to look at in one of her bikinis. The trip would take about a year, and they would stop at some interesting spots, such as Sea Watch on the ocean in Fort Lauderdale, Florida, for Sunday brunch and sample their award-winning lobster Benedict and, of course, have a "Frederico"—a famous Hawaiian frozen cocktail made of Jack Daniel's, Bacardi light rum, pineapple juice, orange juice, passionfruit juice, and guava juice. Since they would never be rushed, they would, of course, stop by their favorite restaurant on the water at Amelia Island named Brett's. They would fill up with their delicious she-crab soup and buy a quart to take with them. Their first stop in Georgia would be at Skipper's on the river and, of course, dine on their scored, deep-fried whole flounder. Their food tour would include oyster Rockefeller in Savannah, Georgia, fresh tuna in Virginia Beach, fresh blue crabs in Chesapeake

Bay, and, of course, lots and lots of Maine lobster. They would use their fourteen-foot dinghy to go ashore at various ports to explore areas of interest, especially in Maine.

Next, it was Wilder's turn to reveal his plan to spend some of his new fortunes, and it was to revisit the British Virgin Islands and purchase a small beach bungalow similar to the one he had seen when he and five friends went on a sailing trip on a truly dream vacation. BS said he had never visited the BVI and asked Wilder what made these islands so special. Wilder still had some photos he had saved on his phone and shared some scenes from the fifteen islands they visited out of the fifty that made up the entire BVI. The islands were volcanic and rose out of the clear, bluish-green water. He had gotten PADI certified in scuba diving prior to his trip, which was an open water diver course completed at St. Simons Island, Georgia. He had his checkout dive at Crystal River, Florida, where he was able to feed and pet manatees weighing several tons. He knew he wanted to scuba dive in the BVI after watching a film of the underwater life of colorful coral and fish that were red, green, purple, and yellow and were abundant on the reefs.

His BVI adventure began at Tortola, where the group leased a fifty-five-foot sailboat from the moorings and sailed to their first island stop. On the way, they made fresh piña coladas and were celebrating on the bow of the boat while their captain, who they had given the nickname "Captain Tranquil" or CT for short, was at the wheel on the stern. All was perfect until CT's brother noticed that he was not at the wheel anymore but in the sea and treading water. After a daring sea rescue, CT explained that he had decided to take a much-needed pee and went down two steps when a rogue wave bounced him overboard—what a way to start an adventure! As they got underway again, the next project was to organize provisions they had purchased at the grocery store named "The Ample Hamper."

The first stop was Virgin Gorda, with its bright green mountains surrounded by some of the clearest and greenest water on earth. They had done their research and knew that a must-see would be the famed baths, which were massive granite boulders that sheltered sea pools on the beach's edge. On the first snorkeling trip around the reef, they saw their first multicolored fish and brilliant coral. After this excursion, they cruised to the north end around Mosquito Island and into Leverick Bay. Tropical drinks were made with fresh pineapple, tuna was put on the grill located on the rail on the stern, and, of course, the reggae song "Red, Red Wine" was played over and over!

Their next stop would be Anegada, a seventeen-mile trip northeast to the most unique of the BVI, the only one formed of limestone and coral. The snorkeling was excellent at Loblolly Bay, and lobster was abundant. They immediately made reservations at an island restaurant to take advantage of freshly caught, grilled lobster. They asked the chef how he prepared the succulent lobster they had read about, and he gave them his recipe: place it in a large pot with boiling water and the seasoning of like a shrimp boil for three minutes, remove it, take out all the meat from the tail and claws, smother it in garlic butter, and put it on the grill over medium heat for six minutes and *bam*! The best lobster you ever ate is served!

Another island they visited was Cave Garden Bay, which had colorful houses on the hillside, most a bright pink and turquoise. They found Quito's Gazebo and enjoyed more tropical drinks and live reggae music. The next morning, they visited their most favorite of all the BVI, Jost Van Dyke Great Harbor. It is home to the legendary Foxy's bar, a favorite for the locals because of the tasty rum drinks at a cheap price. Next, they headed to White Bay to take care of an item on their bucket list—the Soggy Dollar bar known for its famous drink called the "Painkiller."

Their last island visited was Norman Island with its well-protected, scenic bay called the Bight. This area included Treasure Point, where caves abound and are believed to have been used by pirates in the 1800s. Their final day was spent snorkeling over the reefs, and they celebrated with their final island lunge at Pirates Bight. They were out of money, had extended their waistlines somewhat, reluctantly returned to their sailboat, and began their journey home. BS grinned and told Wilder that he now understood why this place had made such a lasting impression—he may go someday himself!

CHAPTER 7

The Search for Gold

Wilder now believed he had enough knowledge to begin his search for treasure on Cumberland Island. He had an extensive history of the island given to him by BS, and valuable information was given to him by a Carnegie descendent and also from a gifted naturalist. He had access to all the island and could explore anywhere on the island without any interference from the Park Service. He had been given a "clearance certificate" by the National Park Service because he was a fishing guide employed by the owners of Greyfield Inn. He was given permission to search for the two lost forts on the island, Fort St. Andrews on the north end and Fort Prince William on the south. He had received a grant from the University of Georgia Historical Society to search for any artifacts at these sites. He also had in his possession two very old, tattered treasure maps showing where treasure may be hidden. He was disappointed that he never located the third map. It had simply disappeared.

Wilder decided to begin his search on the north end of the island called "High Point" to find the star-shaped fort

General Oglethorpe ordered to be built in 1736. His first crude map had directions to proceed thirty paces from the tip of the point of the star located furthest north. Could this be the fort that was star-shaped? He unstrapped his Minelab Excalibur 1100 metal detector from his four-wheeler and wondered if this huge investment of $1,700 was worth it. He had no clue where the old fort was located, so he chose an area at High Point that overlooked St. Andrews Sound and began his search. After an eight-hour search, he had only found a few modern coins and decided to try another area.

The next day, he decided to search the site of Fort Prince William located on the island's south end. He had learned that this fort had been destroyed in 1742 by a Spanish Armada of fifty ships and two thousand soldiers, who sailed from Havana, Cuba. After only twenty minutes of using a metal detector, he heard a high-pitched noise coming from the device, indicating he had found a rather large object. Could this be the gold treasure? He dug with his shovel and used his small handheld device to locate a large black cannonball that later he learned weighed 32 pounds. It was determined to be an artifact from around the 1700s. It had rust that was later removed and determined to be a single-shot cannonball that was used for centuries before giving way to rifled-shot cannon during the American Civil War. This rare find was one of a kind, but he had his sights on objects that shined like gold. He would turn in his find to the Coastal Society Historical Board and return the next day to resume treasure hunting.

Wilder got an early start the next day at the same site, but after two hours of searching, things looked bleak until that wonderful scream was music to his ears. He dug into the black sand 3 feet and used his handheld probe to locate an object that was not black but more like a gold color. Could this be the gold he was looking for? He quickly began to uncover it, and there it was—a brass handle from a broken sword. Emotions were running wild—excitement, enthusiasm, and disappointment all happening at the same time. The blade of the sword was missing, but he knew he had a piece of history and carefully placed it in the waterproof canvas bag he had hung on his four-wheeler. He could hear his heart pounding as he continued to scan the ground, and five minutes later, more sounds were being emitted from the metal detector, and in one hour, he had found an old rusty musket, a pistol, and six brass buttons, but no gold. In his excitement, he had forgotten to put on insect repellent, and sand gnats were mad at him for digging in the dirt they were resting in, and he sprayed himself with DEET-flavored Off, but he had already been bitten about 437 times. He decided to call it a day and return the next day, wearing long pants, a long-sleeved shirt, and his Jungle Jim hat with a protective net attached to it.

He started his search at sunrise the next day and was glad he had changed his attire and had already sprayed himself all over to keep those flying monsters at bay. They were actually worse than the previous day, but besides being hot, he could continue his search. One more button was found in the next three hours, but he had that undeniable feeling he was searching in the right place. Finally, he heard his favorite sound and began digging until he saw something that was large and rusty and quickly realized it was a chain. He pulled on it, but it was buried so deep that he kept digging for 5 feet, and then he saw a sight that astonished him. The chain was attached to a cannon that had been buried by sand over the years. He knew he had made a find of a lifetime and decided to go to Maggie's cabin and tell her and ask what she would do if she had found it. He quickly changed into shorts and a T-shirt and ran wide open until he slid sideways into Maggie's front yard. She came out of her cabin, where she had been dissecting a turtle, cursing him for tearing up the grass in her yard. He told her he was sorry, and if she fetched both of them a beer, he would share a fascinating story with her. She was all in as they sat on the porch, and he related his most recent find. He had found a whole cannon and wondered what else was buried with it. She wanted to see it for herself, and a plan was made for the two of them to each ride there four-wheelers to the site.

Upon arrival, she was amazed at the size of the big gun and told her friend that they should continue searching the site before telling anyone else. They would dig and explore until dark, and Wilder would spend the night at her cabin, and both would return and begin searching at sunrise. She told him he needed a shower in the worst way and directed him to the outdoor shower that produced only ice-cold water from her artesian well. After the shower, he would need to be rubbed all over with alcohol because he now had 562 sand gnat bites as well as some red bumps on his feet from fire ants he had inadvertently stepped in while digging. Wilder asked her to join him in the shower so she could wash his back, and in less than one minute, she was buck naked and calling for the coward to join her. Later, as they relaxed in bed after his rubdown, Wilder wondered if she would mind a kiss. He decided he would rather beg forgiveness than ask permission. She didn't mind at all!

Wilder awoke at 5:00 a.m. because he heard pans rattling, and the aroma of bacon, eggs, and coffee filled the cabin. He slid on his shorts and saw Maggie with her big smile, putting enough eggs, bacon, grits, and toast on his plate for three grown men. She had about the same on her plate and announced this would be the big meal of the day, and they would need all the energy they could muster for their big dig. She asked him how he liked his coffee, and he said, "Just the way I like my women—tan and sweet!"

The sun was just rising over the ocean when they got to their dig site, and from the looks of the gigantic red ball rising, they knew it was going to be another hot day. They began their detecting and digging, but the cannon and chain were all they found. Wilder ventured about 15 feet from the cannon site and got a loud screech from the machine and started digging deeper and deeper until suddenly the ground gave way, and he disappeared. Maggie saw this happen and got to the hole to see Wilder lying on his butt in an open area about 20 feet by 40 feet. Both knew immediately they had found the fort that disappeared in the eighteenth century. She pulled the four-wheeler close to the opening of the hole and lowered the rope from the winch down to Wilder to get him back to safety. He declined and told her to join him and bring the metal detector with her. She lowered it first then herself to the open room, and the two looked at one another, and both started laughing at the same time. They could not believe their new discovery and decided to explore for just a few minutes before going back out. Bones were found, which she identified as belonging to a horse, and the remnants of a wagon were nearby. A cannon with a chain attached to it, a dead horse, and a wagon—what the heck did this all mean?

Giant old logs held this structure together and looked to be cut from large live oak trees. Neither could hardly breathe as they searched the fort until they found three old muskets, a pistol, six silver coins, and a sword as they swept the floor with the metal detector. They heard a noise neither could identify, and Wilder said it was probably the ghost of a soldier who died in a battle fought there. Maggie did not find this funny at all. A plan was made to go back up and make a plan when they were back on top. Another loud noise startled them as they shimmied up the rope, and both made it out where they welcomed the bright sunlight. They both knew this event was much too complicated for the two of them to handle, and both agreed to contact the Coastal Georgia Historical Society and let them take over this project with their crew and equipped with the latest laser technology. A deal was made to keep their find and let that be their secret to be secured at her cabin. They later learned during the excavation that the scientists found three more cannons, twelve muskets, numerous pistols and swords, no gold or silver, and the same dead horse. Work continued, and Wilder and Maggie were awarded nice plaques for their historical discovery.

CHAPTER 8

North-End Gold Search

Maggie had to leave the island and told Wilder she was not sure how long she would be gone, perhaps several months. She asked him to check on her cabin when he could, and she had already given all her animals to one of her neighbors. He later found out she was going to Atlanta, and rumor was she would be spending some time at Emory Hospital. He respected her privacy and told her to let him know if he could do anything, and she replied, "I've got this."

Since the south end of Cumberland was still buzzing with activity from the fort discovery, he made a plan to concentrate on the north end—maybe find another fort but with more treasure in it this time. The five silver coins he and Maggie had found on the south end were seated silver dollars, and the most valuable was the 1848, worth $650 in VF 20 condition. The total value of the five was $2,700, and only he and Maggie knew where they were buried in her backyard. They had both agreed that if either one had an emergency and needed quick cash, these would be used by either party. He now needed a new partner to help him because his buddy Mark was working full-time at Cabin Bluff. He decided to call Mac, his new friend he had met at Greyfield Inn, and see if she had time to join him on his adventure. She agreed to meet him at the inn and invited him to stay for a few days if he could. Of course, he said yes, and the two met the next day and rode double on his four-wheeler to the north end of the island. She pointed out that some areas of Cumberland had eroded, but others had gotten larger and taller with the accumulation of sand because of hurricanes and storms. She recommended they use the technique of "run and gun" and cover lots of territories instead of spending too much time in any one spot.

Her theory as to why this area was called the "Treasure Coast" was related to the recent find of twenty-two silver coins found in the surf with each one dating back to a shipwreck 305 years ago. Twelve Spanish galleons loaded with treasure from the new world were bound for Spain, but on July 31, 1715, eleven were lost in a hurricane off the coast of Florida and perhaps Georgia. It is believed that not all this treasure lives deep in the ocean, and lots of it is in shallow water. Not many artifacts have been found from the 1715 wrecks, but since anyone can search public beaches without a permit, it is feasible that a find worth millions of dollars could happen any day.

With new enthusiasm, Wilder powered up his metal detector, and he and his lovely assistant spent the next three days getting sunburns and bug bitten. Nothing significant was found except some modern-day coins with a JFK half dollar dated 1968 the top prize. Wilder needed a break, and a trip was planned for the next day on the water and ending with dinner at the historic Jekyll Hotel. He surprised her when he docked the sleek forty-two-foot boat with a cuddy cabin at the ferry dock and explained one of his fraternity brothers let him use it while he was out of town on business. The boat named "Sea-Duction" was kept at St. Simons Morningstar Marina, and the owner there had it "showroom" clean and had stocked the bar with top-shelf liquor. He figured this would be ideal for Mac to have as a nice place to shower and change from her daily outfit to her black cocktail dress for their dinner date. Mac was dressed for the day in very tight jeans and a pink long-sleeved Columbia fishing shirt. He explained that the temperature that day would be in the mid-90s, but she said "not to worry" because she had on her yellow bikini under her clothes. She explained that this was not her first rodeo, and she had even packed her black dress in her travel bag. She laughed at the name on the boat and asked if it was his intention. His response was that a captain never ruled out anything on the water, and he was innocent until proven guilty. The float plan was to start at Amelia Island for some sightseeing, shopping, and maybe grab a "Pirate's Punch" at the Palace Saloon on Main Street.

The seas were calm, and the sky was blue as they slowly motored down the ICW toward Florida. They passed the giant submarine base named King's Bay and had a discussion about while it was good for the local economy, many environmentalists worried about the negative effect it might have on Cumberland. They passed the north then the south jetties and tied up at the city dock in Fernandina Beach, Florida. They strolled down Main Street and went into several shops that displayed exquisite jewelry made from the bones of sea creatures, and other items often found on the beach. Wilder was impressed and wondered out loud how anyone could design such works of art. At the finest of the shops, the owner saw Mac and hugged her while explaining that she had sold over 75 percent of the jewelry items Mac had provided her on consignment. Wilder then remembered that Mac was the designer, and this was her work they were viewing. She introduced Wilder as her "charter captain and guide," and she only hung around him because he had a "big boat." As they left and headed to the Palace Saloon, he slapped her on the butt and told her he would get her back for her smart ass comments.

One potent Pirate's Punch was enough, and next, they went to Brett's, a favorite restaurant on the water where both shared fried softshell crabs and peel and eat shrimp. They left and decided to go around Cumberland on the ocean side around the north jetties. Mac insisted they fish for a couple of hours because she had always wanted to catch a tarpon and keep a scale for a piece of jewelry after a photo was taken—first, she had to catch one. Wilder got the rigs ready as he located a large school of menhaden near the beach. He threw his cast net and had a five-gallon bucket full that he emptied into the live bait well. Meanwhile, Mac had disappeared below in the cabin to "freshen up" and greeted her captain wearing an itty-bitty yellow polka dotless bikini that fit her perfectly. She asked for some sunscreen, and the captain started rubbing her legs, and she twisted his ears and said, "Whoa, cowboy, just hit the back where I can't reach," but he played deaf and kept putting more SPF 30 on her legs. After finishing, he asked her to return the favor, and he removed his Columbia fishing shirt that had on the back, "Hickory Bluff Fishing

Club—a drinking village with a fishing problem!" She quit when his back had an ample amount of lotion on it, and he told her if she didn't finish, she would not fish—that didn't work. She noticed a large scar on his shoulder, and he told her he had been attacked by a Great White shark while scuba diving in the British Virgin Islands (when actually, it was a scar from surgery to remove a skin cancer when he was eighteen).

A hand-sized pogie was hooked through the eyes and tossed 30 feet from the boat as the captain strapped on a fighting belt around Mac's waist, and she told him he had twenty minutes to get it done. He liked that, and before he could comment, the rod bent, the drag began screaming, and a giant hundred-plus-pound silver monster went airborne as Mac hung on for dear life. Long runs and eight more acrobatic jumps were made before the silver lady was boat side, one silver-dollar-size scale removed, several pictures taken, and catch and release went perfectly! The captain told her she had just caught the largest tarpon he had ever seen, and after measuring it, his estimate was 150 pounds, and she gave him a big hug that he enjoyed immensely.

While he was putting up the fishing gear, the captain heard a loud splash and saw Mac in the ocean, daring him to join her unless he was scared some little bitty shark might bite him again. He dove in and dunked her in the clear, green water of the Atlantic Ocean. Horses on the beach of Cumberland seemed to be watching them as they swam and played in the water. After returning to the boat, they hosed each other with fresh water and decided to get a little sun on their white bodies. A plan was made to take a shower and go by boat to the Jekyll hotel for the special of the day—surf and turf. She insisted that she had to finish her Mich Ultra and e-mail her prize catch photo to her jewelry shop manager so she could have it printed and framed when she returned. She did it and decided to shower first while the captain did his job—clean up the bloody mess in the boat! The captain knew his first mate was in a good mood because he could hear her singing in the shower one of his favorite Jimmy Buffett songs, "I like mine with lettuce and tomato, / Heinz 57 and french fried potatoes, / Big kosher pickle and a cold draft beer, / Well, good God almighty which way do I steer?" She was definitely one happy lady!

Not to be outdone, as soon as the shower stopped, the captain bellowed out his favorite, "Brandi, you're a fine girl, / What a good wife you would be, / But my life, my lover is the sea!"

She heard him and replied, "Brandi wears a braided chain, / Made of finest silver from the North of Spain, / A locket that bears the name, / Of the man that Brandi loves!" They both started laughing at each other's off-key voices.

Mac emerged from the cabin with a surprise. Her black cocktail dress was red and was complemented with gold starfish earrings and a large gold sand-dollar necklace. She explained the legend of the sand dollar, and that if you break it open, five doves will always emerge representing peace and joy. He wasn't listening to her story but was mesmerized by her beauty, and she asked him if the cat had gotten his tongue. He put his eyes back into his eye sockets and stumbled down the steps to get dressed for the evening.

When he came up, he looked spiffy in his long-sleeved pink Columbia shirt, white trousers, and, of course, a pair of OluKai flip-flops. She gave him a "thumbs-up" on his outfit but pleaded with him to wear the nice alligator loafers instead of the flops to complete his handsome look. He reluctantly agreed and fired up the engines and was docked in front of the Jekyll Hotel in only twenty minutes. They walked past the Wharf Restaurant on the way to the elegant hotel built in 1887. He explained the hotel was made a historic landmark in 1978 and opened as the Radisson Jekyll Island Hotel in 1985. When initially built, it served the needs of society's elite—the Astors, Rockefellers, Goulds, Morgans, and now, today, this stunning couple! Architect Charles A. Alexander was commissioned to design and build a sixty-room clubhouse as well as six additional buildings, which are known today as America's first condominiums.

As the stylish couple entered the front door, Mac immediately noticed the dark, elegant woodwork and rich surroundings of the foyer. A gentleman was playing "Georgia on My Mind" as they walked by to be seated. Mac whispered to the captain if she could sing her favorite song after dinner at the piano, and he laughed and said, "Sure, break a leg," remembering her off-key shrill voice earlier. Drink orders were taken, and Wilder got his usual Grey Goose extra dry martini, and she ordered a Long Island iced tea, which was made with vodka, gin, tequila, rum, triple sec, and cola. She told her companion to limit her to just one, and he just shook his head. Both ordered the "surf and turf," which consisted of prime rib and lobster. The wine list was presented, and since she was not a wine connoisseur, he asked Mac to choose, and her choice was a 2017 Far Niente Cabernet. As they enjoyed their meal and wine over candlelight, Mac asked Wilder if they could do this once a month, and he told her, of course. All they needed to do was first, find a million-dollar treasure on Cumberland! She said to remind her of a story she heard from her grandmother about a treasure when they returned to the island.

After dinner, they headed back to the boat but stopped when they heard music being played outside and realized that the group called the "Stingrays" was singing "Let's Get It On" by Marvin Gaye. They led each other to the dance floor, where they stayed for four more of these slow, romantic songs to be sung. As they boarded the boat, Wilder made a suggestion that instead of chancing getting a "BUI" (boating under the influence), which would ruin his career as a charter captain, they stay in one of the guesthouses which were part of the hotel where he thought each had two bedrooms if needed. Mac readily agreed but questioned why they would need two bedrooms unless he was scared of her. He secured the cottage and closed the door to the little getaway, and guess what happened? Let's leave that to the reader's imagination!

The next day while unpacking their bags at Greyfield Inn, Wilder asked Mac if she was serious when she said she had heard of a clue about a treasure on the island. She said that she would share some old family secrets that had been passed on during the years from the Carnegie family. They got some sweet tea and enjoyed the rocking chairs on the front porch, where Mac deliberately kept Wilder waiting until he could not stand it anymore. He begged her, and she told him she had second thoughts because he might get the secret and leave and never come back to see her. He replied that as long as she had that sexy red dress and that skimpy yellow bikini, wild horses couldn't keep him away!

She asked him to follow her to the library, where they sat on the antique couch, and she began her story. Her great-great-grandmother kept a diary religiously, and if she saw or heard any interesting gossip, she wrote it down in her private diary. She had earmarked a few pages to share with him but told him the rest was personal family stories and history that would remain family secrets. She related that most everyone outside her family thought since they had mansions, they were immune to problems but actually had their share of family turmoil.

These pages of the diary were the ones that reveal some gold and silver coins that were found in Cumberland many years ago. Thomas Carnegie was her great-great-grandfather, and he told his wife that he had found these coins and even had one made into a necklace for her. Lucy wrote that the necklace was stolen from her jewelry case she kept in her bedroom at Greyfield Inn. She wrote that it was a large twenty-dollar-gold piece that looked brand-new and was admired by everyone who saw it. She pleaded with her husband to give her another one, but he refused because of his stubborn demeanor—no more mention of any coins forever written in her journal. The next time Mac heard of any valuable coins was when her grandmother, Lucy Fergueson, told her about coins owned by her husband, Robert Fergueson. He was an avid coin collector and enjoyed showing his collection to friends, family, and even visitors. His favorites were his gold coins that were in perfect proof condition, and his twenty-dollar-gold Liberty ones were some of his most valuable. He had purchased most of his coins while doing business in Philadelphia, Pennsylvania, and had bought such brilliant specimens as an 1815 five-dollar coin in mint state 67 condition, a 1913-S ten-dollar Indian-head gold coin, and an 1852-O twenty-dollar St. Gaudens in perfect condition. He frequently attended coin shows and was seen as one of the most knowledgeable numismatists in America. He often bragged that he had found more gold and silver coins than he had bought but never elaborated anymore about his treasure hunting.

As he became older, Robert became paranoid and often complained that he suspected someone was planning to steal his collection and always carried a small derringer in his pants pocket. When questioned by Miss Lucy about its whereabouts, he changed his story from "in a bank up north" to "hidden on this island so no one, not even you could find it." He told her if she wanted to play a "cat and mouse game," he would give her any coin she wanted and make it into a necklace for her if she ever found them. He gave her a map that she kept in her diary, and here it is—"Look up, not down, you fool. The gold glitters as bright as the great light imprisoned in mortar, brick, and stone!" Mac gave him a copy of it, and Wilder decided that treasure was a treasure—no matter if the Spanish buried it or ole Robert hid it!

CHAPTER 9

Light at the End of the Tunnel

Wilder read the note over and over but could not reach any conclusion regarding its meaning. The only plan was to keep searching on the north end of the island because the southern end was still being excavated by the archaeologists. Did he make a mistake by telling these professionals about the fort, thus ruining his search for treasure there? He decided to spend the day at the ruins of Dungeness and used his metal detector to look for any artifacts. He thought of buying a drone that would allow him to check out the tall chimneys of the ruins, but that was not in his budget, but tall borrowed ladders would suffice. He kept reciting, "Look up, not down," and wondered if the fire from the chimney could be the light mentioned in the note. He asked Mark to help him, and the two used ladders to give a thorough inspection of the bricks. Their reward was getting covered by black soot and getting attacked by bats, who became mad when their nests were disturbed. They took pictures of each other in their black face and rode to the ocean to clean up before anyone saw them. They were tired, discouraged, and decided to once again depend on their old mentor BS for guidance before they gave up on their project.

BS was at the marina, playing Texas Holdem Poker on his new iPad when the two arrived. BS told the boys they looked like hell and asked what was the black stuff still in their hair and behind their ears? They chuckled and told him about their escapade and asked him to look at the note that led them to their "lookup" venture. BS studied the note for a good five minutes and then told them it didn't take any college education to figure out what it meant. He said ole Robert had described the lighthouse on the north end of Cumberland. Both of them looked at each other, wondering why they had not come up with the same conclusion. The boys were thinking they were both educated way beyond their intelligence!

Wilder, Mac, and Mark decided to focus on the lighthouse and the surrounding area in hopes of finding a treasure above ground. Mac would be their "ticket" in their search because she was a local and could help avoid any confrontation with another island dweller. They organized their canvas bag with flashlights, shovels, picks, bug spray, and the metal detector and its accessories. Each had agreed to split the treasure money evenly and include BS as well. If the treasure was indeed hidden there, where to look was the obvious question. The facts revealed it was built in 1838. It hadn't been functional for many years and was not on land owned by the Park Service. Their story, if anyone asked, was to continue to research the north end for artifacts for historical purposes.

Day 1 was a very hot day with the "no-see-ums" held at bay because of the extreme heat. They each chose an area to search, and Mark would use a metal detector to scan the base of the structure while Mac would search the spiral staircase area and inside around the door and windows. Wilder would concentrate at the top where the light with the Fresnel lens was located. He had been given "lighthouse 101" by BS, who told him this lens was invented by Augustin Fresnel in 1822, and each face of the lens was surrounded by a ring of triangular prisms which reflected and focused the light so it could be seen at a distance of 20 miles in clear weather. The fog was always a hazard and could greatly reduce visibility, so they were frequently equipped with foghorns, bells, or any other sound devices to warn those navigating nearby seas. He added that only about 1,400 lighthouses remain worldwide because of advanced technology and advanced navigational aids. The older ones had 1,000-watt tungsten bulbs, but today, a 250-watt halogen bulb would do the same. More interesting facts were the Greeks and Romans had lighthouses over a thousand years ago and lit fires on the highest land of an island and called them beacon fires. They warned mariners of hazards, helped them establish their position, and guided them to their destination. Next came tall towers that were built with a powerful light at the top, and usually, a keeper's house was also built. The first colonial lighthouse was built in Boston in 1716, first in Florida in 1824, and the Cumberland one in 1838. All these facts reminded Wilder of a poem he had learned in the fifth grade, "On a foggy day, when you hear a whale snoring, it is probably a foghorn blaring. Beware, you are reaching the shore. When the fog fades away, you will see the lights galore!"

Nothing was found the first day, but the trio was excited and ready to begin day two at sunrise. Mac wanted to use the metal detector outside while Mark would investigate the bottom inside. Wilder would go back to the top and scan the area for anything of value. An hour into the search, Mark blew his loud whistle to summon the others to the area he was checking and to show them his discovery. He had noticed a loose block about head high near the spiral staircase, and that's where it was. No, not gold but a small derringer hidden by someone, maybe for self-defense. Both Wilder and Mac immediately thought about the derringer Robert Fergueson kept on his person. Could this be his? Why was it hidden there? Its find gave them new energy, and each returned to their individual search at a slightly faster speed.

Wilder sat in the middle of the room at the top and just looked at his surroundings for thirty minutes. BS had told him, "You can learn a lot just by looking," which he did. He noticed that the base of the giant light had a plate with four screw holes but only three screws. He found this unusual and using his screwdriver, removed the three screws and, with his flashlight, examined the large, dusty area just when he saw it—a spider that looked to weigh a pound and was as big as a fist. He removed it with a pair of pliers and decided not to kill it since it was there first, and he was just a visitor. Another object was at the back of the base out of reach until he used a long crowbar to begin inching it forward to him. Could it be…yes it was…a canvas bag like ones he had seen to contain coins the Mint sold to customers. His adrenaline was pumping. His heart rate was at least a hundred, as he dragged it to him and found it was empty! It did contain ten other small bags that were empty also, and his mind raced as he tried to make sense of his discovery. Had someone found coins and left the bags? Who put them there initially? Was this the collection of Robert Fergueson? He took a deep breath and kept looking in the farthest corner. He spotted another small bag—no, two small bags that were wedged in the seam of the base. He extended his arm and a crowbar as far as he could until he was able to drag them to within reach and immediately knew the small bags were not empty but had...what? Could it be what he hoped for?

In all the excitement, Wilder had forgotten to use his loud "catcall" whistle to alert his team that they needed to move fast to see what he had found. He whistled and then wondered how these bags were still there, and all other bags were empty. He waited until his buddies arrived and then emptied the contents of the small bags on his bandanna and saw two $20 gold coins that he recognized to be of the Liberty type and immediately looked at the dates, and one was an 1850, and the other was in 1852-O. Wilder had the coin book, Greysheet app, on his phone and found that if both were in almost perfect condition, which they appeared, both could be worth close to $500,000! He would have to have the condition verified by a friend who owned a coin shop in Jacksonville, Florida, but he knew a magnificent treasure had been found. But could there be more? A thorough search of the base was conducted as well as the entire light, but nothing else was found except a large, dead rat and two more spiders. Did someone find Robert's coin collection and left these two in a hurry to get the coins and get away? Did Robert leave two coins on purpose and move the rest? What about the derringer that was found hidden? Had it been used in a spoiled robbery?

Since no more coins were found, Wilder took photos of the two and sent them to Andy, who replied that both were MS-65, and he would gladly offer $200,000 for the 1850 and $300,000 for the 1852-O if they agreed right then to a deal. A vote was taken, and 3 to 0, it was agreed to sell them to him for $500,000. They would leave immediately and take them to him, and he would have $500,000 in cash for them when they arrived. They jumped out of the boat at the marina, got into Mark's old Ford F-150, and made the trip via I-95 south to Jacksonville, Florida, in a record fifty-five minutes. The coins were inspected and verified by Andy, and the envelope with the cash was given to the trio. They chatted nonstop about how each would spend their new fortune. Mark would buy a brand new Ford F-150, Mac would buy the shop on St. Simons for her new jewelry store, and Wilder would buy the bungalow he found when he visited the British Virgin Islands. Of course, he had to visit to make sure it was still available, but he didn't want to go alone, and he wished he knew someone who would go with him—preferably an attractive lady. Mac smiled and fluttered her eyes and simply said, "Will I need a passport for our trip?"

CHAPTER 10

Could There Be More Treasure?

Wilder, Mac, and Mark met BS at the marina to update him on their treasure and give him the highlights from what had happened in the last two weeks. He was offered his share of the money from the coins but told them he never planned to take any. He just wanted to help motivate them to find it. He bragged that he had been a genius when he had bought some cheap stocks back before they got popular such as Facebook, Google, and Amazon. He laughed when he asked them if they had ever heard of these stocks, and he now had more money than he could ever spend in his lifetime. His reward would be one of the artifacts, preferably a musket, that he could display in the tackle shop at the marina. He would do research on it, and it would be an interesting addition to the Cumberland Island history class he was teaching at the local college next month.

BS looked at the photos of the two coins the trio found and had a theory about their reason for being at the lighthouse. His research had led him to discover one gentleman who had a very valuable coin collection worth several million dollars, and his name was Robert Fergueson. Wilder winked at Mac because this was the same character Mac's grandmother had told her about from the diary. It was rumored that Robert did not trust banks and had become paranoid and had hidden his collection somewhere away from Greyfield. What better place than the isolated old lighthouse for him to go and look at the coins when he wanted peace and solitude. If this story was fact, not fiction, what happened that caused him to leave the two coins there, and where was the rest of them? Wilder and Mac began thinking about what BS had postulated and would test their theory at a later date. BS asked his friends about their adventures during the last two weeks and told them since he was old as dirt, he could live vicariously from their fun. Mark began and explained that he had come to his senses, and instead of buying a brand-new, loaded, $55,000 Ford F-150 truck, he had bought his uncle's truck and saved a lot of money. He planned to use this money to expand his charter fishing business by investing in a website and a blog.

Wilder was giddy when he started talking about his and Mac's trip to the Virgin Islands. He was immediately interrupted by Mac, who wanted to show BS an item she had "splurged" on—a tattoo of a porpoise in the blue-green BVI water with Jost Van Dyke Island in the background. It was located below her waist on her back when she pulled her shorts down, and BS remarked that the area must have had an earthquake because he swore he saw a crack down there. He got a playful slap for his crude remark, but everyone else got a good laugh from it. Wilder told of a fabulous fishing trip he and Mac had there, and he had caught a 600-plus pound blue marlin while charter fishing on a forty-two-foot Contender named "She Got the House!"

He had sent the photos, length, and girth to a buddy in Miami, Florida, to make a replica for him. His dream was to own a boat like the Contender and use it for offshore fishing trips. He would name his new boat "Mac Attack" and promise each client they would have a special viewing of a BVI tattoo if they left a generous tip. He also got a head slap by the tattoo owner for this smart remark.

The three said goodbye to their favorite captain but knew he would always be their mentor, especially for treasure hunting trips on Cumberland Island. He told them he had one more theory about where Mr. Robert had taken his coins, but he would wait until they picked him up in that forty-two-foot Contender to tell them. They laughed and guaranteed it would happen sooner than later!

As they were getting in the truck to leave, BS asked them if they had heard the news about some virus from China named coronavirus, and they had not. He told them to stay healthy and not get this terrible flu. Hopefully, all stayed healthy.

ABOUT THE AUTHOR

Jimmy lives on the Georgia coast in a small fishing village named Hickory Bluff. Fishing is a major hobby for most of the residents, and he frequently joins them at Hickory Bluff Marina, where boats are launched, fishing lies are told, and good food is eaten. After retiring as a school psychologist, Jimmy obtained his real estate license and is currently a broker/owner of JP Wheeler Properties, specializing in coastal real estate. Two of his favorite hobbies are boating and fishing, especially in and around Cumberland Island. His numerous visits to the island gave him the inspiration to write this book to give the reader some interesting history facts as well as telling a story of fishing and adventure. He lives and works on the coast of the "Golden Isles" with his wife, Burdette, and his dog Herschel.